The WORD in History

The WORD in History

THE ST. XAVIER SYMPOSIUM

Edited by *T. PATRICK BURKE*

SHEED AND WARD : NEW YORK

71018

Contents

Introduction	*vii*
T. PATRICK BURKE	
Theology and Anthropology	*1*
KARL RAHNER	
Nature and Grace	*24*
HENRI DE LUBAC	
Faith Functioning in Human Self-Understanding	*41*
E. SCHILLEBEECKX	
The Principal Problem for Protestant Theology Today	*60*
JOSEPH SITTLER	
The Church and the World	*69*
J. B. METZ	
Christianity and non-Christian Religions	*86*
JEAN DANIÉLOU	
The Framework of Catholic-Protestant Disagreement	*102*
GEORGE A. LINDBECK	
Freedom in the Church	*120*
ALEXANDER SCHMEMANN	

Institutionalized Religion   133
    YVES CONGAR

Understanding the Real Presence   154
    CHARLES DAVIS

Contributors   179

Introduction

The essays which make up this book were originally delivered as papers at a symposium, the purpose of which was to ask a question: What are the principal theological problems facing the Church at the present time?[1] The question was based on a number of premises, the first being that, in general, progress begins with the realization that there is a problem. Failure to see a serious problem where it exists can quickly lead to disaster. Yet, frequently it is not at all obvious where the real difficulties lie: they may be obscured by a variety of zealous preoccupations. It is the evidence of history that the Church has not always seen the most important problems that were confronting her. A classic instance of this is surely the Fifth Lateran Council, defining the immortality of the human soul on the eve of the Reformation, apparently unaware that it was sitting on a powder keg with the fuse already burning. In our own day I think we have come to realize that the historical form of the liturgy had already become a serious problem by the sixteenth century, and contained elements which unnecessarily impeded the full growth of the Church's life; yet it is only recently that this was recognized sufficiently that something was done about it.

This volume then must be considered, not as a presentation of ready-made solutions, but as an inquiry: Are we asking the right questions? Where are our principal difficulties?

The inquiry takes its specific character from another premise also: namely, that the problems which face the Church are not only, or even primarily, of what is called a "practical" nature, such as how to organize the activities of a parish or diocese most efficiently. No one can deny that the Church is confronted with urgent questions of this kind; but it is also true that the effectiveness of the Church, as the presence of Christ in and among men, can be very seriously, perhaps most seriously, impeded by her failure (which is our failure) to solve problems of what is called a "theoretical" nature. The Church lives from the Word of God; she exists to embody and proclaim the Christian gospel. It is a matter of vital importance for us, then, as Christians and members of the Church to ascertain what precisely *is* the Christian gospel, how we are to understand the Word of God in our day and age. Practice which is not based explicitly or implicitly on sound theory is impractical, and in the long run it will hinder rather than build up the work of God. The inquiry presented here then is specifically *theological* inquiry.

As theological inquiry which is Christian, it must be ecumenical; and here there is a third premise on which it rests, which may be stated as follows. Ecumenical theology does not consist simply in people of different beliefs explaining their beliefs to one another; nor does it consist in carrying on a theology which would be, for example, neither Catholic nor Protestant. Rather, the task of the Catholic theologian is to help construct a Catholic theology, one which will be faithful to truly Catholic principles and acceptable to his fellow Catholics, but one which incorporates all that which is acceptable in the position of his partner in dialogue, the Protestant or Orthodox. And the Protestant, on his part, must carry on a theology which will be faithful to Protestant principles, acceptable to his fellow Protestants, but one which incorporates that which can be accepted from the Catholic position—in the hope that one day, by the grace of God, we may find ourselves together. In one word, ecumenical theology, being based on faith, must be unashamedly *confessional*. This book, then, is concerned specifically with advancing Catholic theology, precisely because it is intended to be ecumenical. However, the reader will scarcely fail to perceive the almost astonishing depth of unity in outlook underlying the Catholic and non-Catholic contributions.

The subject-matter of the various papers was decided upon as follows. Each of the Catholic contributors was asked what, in his opinion, were the principal problems facing Catholic theology today. The curious fact emerged of an almost total agreement in their answers, and the topics treated here represent this consensus. That each of these topics, then, constitutes an urgent question is not simply the private opinion of the author, but of the other contributors also: which is not to say that there may not be considerable disagreement among them as to how the particular questions ought to be answered. 'And here again the reader will also see how closely the contributions of the non-Catholic participants fit in with the Catholic ones—without there having been any such prior intention.

The papers presented here, then, are not meant to give definitive answers. but to point out problems that must be dealt with. They will fulfill their function best if they are taken as a starting point, a stimulant to the creative thinking which is needed if the Church is to preach the Gospel effectively to the world in which she lives and of which she forms a part.

I would like to take this occasion to thank warmly all those who contributed to the success of the symposium itself. I believe I can say, on behalf of all who attended, that it was an excellent example of the Word as Event.

T. PATRICK BURKE

NOTES

1 "The Theological Task Confronting the Church Today," held at Saint Xavier College, Chicago, March 31st to April 3rd, 1966, under the auspices of the John XXIII Institute.

The WORD in History

KARL RAHNER

Theology and Anthropology

It is the purpose of this essay to show that dogmatic theology today has to be theological anthropology, and that such an anthropocentric orientation of theology is both necessary and fruitful. That is, the question of man, and the answer to this question, should not be considered a separate area, distinct from the other areas of theological inquiry. It must be looked upon, rather, as the whole of dogmatic theology. Such a thesis does not involve any contradiction to the theocentric nature of all theology, to St. Thomas's teaching, for example, that God is the formal object of theology. As soon as man is understood as that being which has absolute transcendence toward God (and it is surely obvious that he is such) then anthropocentricity and theocentricity in theology are not contradictories but strictly one and the same thing seen from two different aspects, and each aspect is unintelligible without the other. That theology should be anthropocentric does not contradict its being most rigorously theocentric: it is, however, opposed to the view that man is merely one particular topic in theology among others, for example, the angels or the material world. It is contrary to the view that it is possible to speak theologically about God without at the same time saying something about man, and vice versa. Speech about God and speech about man are connected, not only from

1

the point of view of content, but from the point of view of knowledge itself.

It is not possible to explain more precisely here just why such a theology, centered on man, is not in opposition to a theology centered on Christ. Let us say just this—in Christian dogmatic theology there is a mutual and necessary relationship between anthropology and Christology, if these are both rightly understood. Christian anthropology only attains its full meaning when it conceives of man as the obediential potency for the hypostatic union. And on the other hand we can develop a Christology today only from the standpoint of such a transcendental anthropology. If, for example, we want to talk about the hypostatic union without incurring suspicion that we are propounding irrelevant myths, we must make it clear that there is in the graced nature itself of man and of his history a transcendental horizon[1] for the idea of a God-man. A Christology which is developed merely a posteriori cannot be integrated into a comprehensive evolutionary understanding of the world and cannot escape the suspicion of being mythology.

I.

Such an anthropology must, of course, be a transcendental anthropology. Transcendental questioning asks about a thing from the point of view of the necessary conditions *in the subject itself* that make it possible for that thing to be known or done by the subject concerned. Such questioning presupposes that the knowing subject is not simply a thing among other things, in such a way that one can indeed speak about it on occasion if one will, but that in other statements about other things it is not even implied. If I make a statement about Australia, I have not said anything about Java, even implicitly. But I have said something implicitly in this statement both in the content of the statement and in the very act of saying it, about man as knower, as the person who makes the statement. For the statement to be possible, certain necessary conditions in man himself are presupposed and are therefore implicitly affirmed in the statement.

If you wish to carry on dogmatic theology as transcendental anthropology then in every dogmatic question you examine you must seek to discover the conditions in man, the knowing subject, himself which make it possible for him to arrive at knowledge of the matter in question: you must prove that there are such a priori conditions for the knowledge of this object, and further you must show that these very conditions are such that they themselves already imply and affirm something about the *object*, its character, its limits and the method by which it is known. Transcendental inquiry does not presume that the total reality of the object examined can be deduced from the transcendental conditions in the subject for knowledge of it nor does it presume that that aspect of the object which is known a posteriori is unimportant for the knowing subject, for his existence, (his "salvation"), and the truth of his knowledge. The same is true in theology; for example, in Christology it is not only important to see man as a creature inwardly directed by his very being (which has been supernaturally elevated and oriented by grace) toward an absolute Savior. It is just as important for his salvation that he actually encounter Jesus of Nazareth as this Savior which, of course, cannot be "transcendentally deduced."

The interpretation of dogmatic theology as transcendental anthropology does, however, demand that every theological question must also be considered from a transcendental point of view. One must ask oneself the question then also what this implicitly affirmed structure of the theological subject himself reveals concerning the object known a posteriori (from the history of salvation and revelation). Of course, the problem of the relationship between a theology which is transcendental and a priori and one which is historical or a posteriori is not solved by these observations. In fact, the problem is only seen in its real depth and intensity when one remembers that in theology the ultimate a priori condition, in the subject, of theological knowledge: that is, grace (which in the last analysis is God himself freely acting in history and communicating himself to man)—this ultimate a priori condition is also the real content, the objective basis of that which is historical and is known a posteriori. Hence in theology the a priori element in the knower and the a posteriori historical element in the thing known have a relationship which is quite unique. But this will be discussed again later.

Let us try to clarify what we have just expressed in such abstract concepts with a few simple and arbitrary examples. Theology makes certain statements about angels, basing itself on the Old and New Testaments. The traditional theology of the schools speaks of these angels as it does of any other matters. Something has been revealed about them in the scriptures: therefore, angels exist. And so, gathering and systematizing the data from the scriptures, we can come to speak about angels just as we speak about anything else we know of. If, by chance, God had not revealed this, there would be no theology about angels. But God was pleased to reveal this, just as he could have revealed innumerable other facts still hidden from us. He could, for example, have revealed whether there are spiritual corporeal beings with "sanctifying" grace on other planets, but He did not. For this reason we now have a theology about angels, but no theology about extraterrestrial, corporeal beings with intelligence. The man of today will ask first of all why these strange tidings about the angels should be any concern of his when he never really encounters such beings in the sphere of his scientific experience, why God should have given us such information, and whether such a thing is really credible. The strangeness of the message will impel him to investigate how the alleged revelation took place. He will then be tempted to show that the Old Testament statements about angels (on which the New Testament statements depend) do not seem to have been communicated to us from heaven, but rather appear to have originated in the heads of the Old Testament theologians under the influence of their spiritual and religious milieu. In this situation of tension between the traditional theology of angels and an attitude of scepticism and doubt about them a transcendental theological anthropology must now come forward. That is to say, we must ask the question: at what point in man's theological understanding of himself can something like the theology of angels be relevant? In other words, what sort of theological understanding of himself does man reveal when he speaks about angels? If we make the heuristic assumption that revelation tells man what he himself is, in his origin, his present condition, and his destiny, that it tells him this and really only this— then how can we explain why such a revelation should be concerned with angels? Could it be that the really significant matter in revelation is not the existence and nature of angels as such, but rather man's relationship to them as creatures whose existence is simply taken for granted? And here the question can remain open as to whether in a revelation oriented toward man the existence of angels is specifically affirmed or whether it appears there merely as a hypothesis. We are not attempting here to elucidate how and to what extent a doctrine of angels can be developed from such a point of departure. The foregoing example was only intended to show what we mean by a dogmatic theology which is oriented toward and centered upon man.

Let us take a further example. The doctrine of the Trinity does not seem to be one that can be easily deduced from scripture itself, in exact biblical theology. Moreover, when it is propounded in a purely objective fashion, the person hearing it not infrequently asks himself what it means, how he can possibly understand anything of it, why it was revealed for his salvation. For it strikes him as a subtle, dialectical play of ideas in which each statement seems to cancel out the next, leaving only words, unless when you make one statement you forget what the other one said, and so give a meaning to the first statement which the dialectical opposition involved does not allow. I take it that I need not explain this impression any further. We cannot get ourselves out of the difficulty merely by alluding to the fact that we are dealing with a mystery and by saying that the doctrine of the Trinity is necessary in order to be able to speak about Christ. For even with a mystery it must be understood why there is more in question than merely a sacrifice of our intellect to a formula of apparently unintelligible verbalism. Nor is the appeal to Christology alone convincing, if we reflect that scholastic theology since Augustine has unhesitatingly maintained that *each* of the divine persons could enter into a hypostatic union with human nature. By that token therefore, theology hardly seems to have said very much, from the point of view of content, even when it stresses that the divine incarnation comes about precisely through the Logos. For under such presuppositions the hypostatic function of the Logos is in no way distinct from a similar possible function of one of the other divine persons. But if we understand the doctrine of the Trinity anthropocentrically, many aspects of it become clearer, even though, of course, the mystery still remains. This is quite possible. All we need to do is to make the quite legitimate assumption that because God communicates himself absolutely to us in uncreated grace what we call the immanent Trinity is strictly identical with the trinity of roles which we find in salvation history *(die ökonomische Trinität),* and vice versa, then it is quite possible for us to understand the Trinity "anthropologically" without distorting it. This results if we make the following assumptions, namely that the direct relationship to God which is given us through grace (including its appearance in salvation history) has a trinitarian structure, that this relationship is always a relationship to the incomprehensible God, that it is communicated through God's historical and absolute commitment of himself to man in Jesus, that this commitment of himself without losing anything of its divineness, truly enters into the very heart of our being in the form of love. And if we presuppose, as we have said, that the trinitarian structure of this immediate relationship to God in grace also belongs to "God in himself" because God is truly giving himself to man—if we make these assumptions, then an understanding of the enduring mystery of the interior life of the Trinity is possible which no longer gives the impression of being a mere game with words, and it becomes possible for us to understand why this mystery had to be revealed at that precise moment when the history of revelation had progressed to the point where it became clear that the ultimate gift of salvation is not only a gift which God makes, but is God himself. There is also no disadvantage in the fact that such a conception of the Trinity also implies that our relationship to the three divine persons by grace is not mere appropriation; that the divinization of man by grace is more clearly connected with the incarnation than the theology of the schools usually teaches. And if in such a conception it is quite impossible for the impression to be given —an impression which the scholastic doctrine of the Trinity scarcely ever avoids, despite its explicit rejection of it—the impression namely that each divine person has his own center of consciousness in knowledge and freedom and that this is the real meaning of the word "person" even in the doctrine of the Trinity—if this impression cannot be given here, then this can only be a commendation of the suggested approach. I repeat I am not attempting here to develop a doctrine of the Trinity.

I am simply using an example to suggest what the approach of transcendental anthropology might mean for all the topics of dogmatic theology.

II.

Because of the lack of time we must be satisfied with these two arbitrary examples. Now we must ask the basic question: why is such an anthropological approach to theology necessary? There are reasons based on the nature of theology and of its object, and there are reasons arising from fundamental theology and apologetics.

1. In the first place, let us consider the reasons which arise from the nature of the case. It is of the essence of all knowledge (including, therefore, theological knowledge) that an inquiry regarding an object of knowledge is also an inquiry regarding the being of the knowing subject. This unavoidable link between the objective and the subjective side of knowledge does not have to be treated explicitly in every science, of course. Natural science, for example, as such, does not have to carry on natural philosophy, which is or implies an inquiry concerning the being of the subject who can and must carry on natural science. But where any particular branch of science becomes really philosophical (and theology must of its very nature be such) every question about any of its objects formally implies a question about the knowing subject. For on the one hand, a question is philosophical if it inquires formally about a particular object with regard to its place in the whole of reality and truth, because only such an inquiry is an inquiry into ultimate causes and, therefore, philosophical. If such an inquiry is carried out, then the knowing subject is not inquired about only *implicitly*, because it happens to be a material part of the whole. The knowing subject *must* be inquired about, since it is only in the subject himself as such, because of his own subjective indi-

viduality, that the whole has meaning, as that towards which his transcendentality is directed. Philosophical inquiry concerning a particular object is necessarily an inquiry concerning the knowing subject because it is the subject who must bring with him a priori the horizon for the possibility of such knowledge. And by that very fact the "transcendental" structure of the object is already implied a priori. Now a theological question can only be asked if it is understood at the same time as a philosophical question in this sense, for a question is theological only if it sees the individual object in its origin and destiny in God. But God is not simply one object among others in the a posteriori experience of man, he is the original basis and the absolute future of all reality. As such, however, he can only be considered as the absolute goal towards which man's transcendentality is directed: all such theology, therefore, is necessarily transcendental anthropology. All *Onto*-logy is Onto-*logy*. If one does not wish to fall into a heretical, positivistic fideism, then one must maintain the same thing about theology: for the unlimited transcendental horizon of the human spirit, which alone makes such an idea as that of God possible, is an inner element of theology itself and the condition which makes it possible. "Natural" theology is from first to last not an occupation carried on alongside theology based on revelation, as if the two could be carried on independently of one another: natural theology is an inner element in revelation theology itself.

The thesis which is in question here, however, can be supported more directly with theological arguments. In the first place, revelation is revelation for salvation, and therefore, theology is essentially theology for salvation. It is not just anything which is revealed, and then considered in theology, but only that which serves the salvation of man. This sentence is not a principle which would allow us automatically to exclude certain objects from the ambit of a possible revelation (as a certain type of fundamentalism imagines), for it is only from revelation itself that we discover what constitutes salvation. But the statement must nevertheless be taken seriously. Only that can belong to salvation of which the absence would injure the being of man and so destroy him. This is no rationalistic or unhistorical reduction of man as a theological being to an abstract transcendental being as if that which is historical and concrete and experienced a posteriori had no significance for his salvation. But it does mean that everything which has significance for man's salvation must be related to his transcendental being, which is not to say that it can be deduced from it. Perhaps an example will make the matter a little clearer. The concrete person who is loved by me, through whom my love is actualized and without whom it cannot exist, cannot possibly be deduced from the a priori possibility of man. Rather, such a person is an historical event which cannot be reduced to any prior factors. But, nevertheless, this love for this concrete person is only properly understood when man is understood to be that being who must necessarily realize himself in love in order to correspond to his own being. Even the most incalculable love, the most concrete and historical, must be understood as transcendental in this sense in order to be what it ought to be. This is all the more so when it is a question of salvation, for if this salvation is itself an historical event then it concerns precisely the real being of man. For it is precisely this which is accomplished, either for salvation or destruction. If, therefore, revelation and theology are related essentially to salvation, then this very nature of revelation and of theology demands that an inquiry be made into the being of man, no matter what the particular object of the examination may be, since it is precisely this being of his which must be able to be affected by this object unto salvation. In other words, the significance of a theological question for the salvation of man, which is a necessary element of every theological question, can only be inquired into insofar as one inquires into the receptivity of man for this object from the point of view of his salvation. However, we cannot ask about man's receptivity for an object from the point of view of his salvation simply in the abstract and in general. We must ask about it in reference to the concrete object with which theology is concerning itself in each case. For just as it is man's receptivity to the object which gives it theological significance, so also the object, in a certain sense, specifies this receptivity itself.

In addition to these considerations, however, there is another consideration which may well be decisive. The Council's decree on ecumenism emphasizes that not all dogmas in the "hierarchy" of truths are equally close to the "foundations" of the Christian faith. There is, therefore, according to the Council, a foundation, an inner core to the reality of faith to which all other realities and propositions are related. By the nature of the case, this core can only be God himself insofar as he himself is our salvation through his absolute gift of himself to us and is, therefore, what we usually call in theology "uncreated grace." With the possession of this grace salvation is given, without it salvation is not given. At the very least, therefore, this must belong to the core realities of revelation. If we consider further that the reality of the triune God as such is given with this grace, if it and the Trinity are rightly understood; and if we further take it for granted that this grace is the grace of Christ and that Christ is not only a meritorious cause of it, remaining extrinsic to it (and this includes even the grace given before the fall): then in the history of this grace as God's communication of himself to man, the history of mankind reaches its eschatological climax and becomes irrevocable precisely in Christ. Thus, the Trinity and the incarnation are both implied in the mystery of grace. In this way it becomes understandable that grace does not simply belong to the core reality of revelation and salvation, but *is* this core itself (which, of course, could also be said of the Trinity from the point of view of salvation

history) and which could also be said of Christ as the climax
of God's communication of himself to the world precisely because these three realities mutually imply one another. However, it is quite impossible to speak of this grace meaningfully
outside of a transcendental anthropology. For quite apart from
the fact that this grace is God himself, communicating himself
to man, it is in any event not a thing but precisely as communicated grace a condition of the personal subject which
places him in immediate relationship to God. That reality of
salvation which is most objective is necessarily at the same time
the most subjective, the immediate relationship of the personal
subject to God, through God himself. If what grace is, is not to
be expressed in a verbalism which smacks of mythology and has
no relationship to experience, then it can be grasped only from
the standpoint of the subject, his transcendentality, and his experience of his transcendentality, as a being-caught-up-into the
reality of absolute truth *(Verwiesenheit in die Realität der
absoluten Wahrheit)*, as a love freed for infinite and absolute
validity, as an immediate relationship to the absolute mystery of
God, in short as an absolute fulfillment of the transcendentality
of man himself, made possible by God in communicating himself to man so that man may be united with him.

Without an ontology of the transcendental subject, the theology of grace and, therefore, theology itself remains in a stage
of pre-theological imagery and cannot take up the approach
offered by transcendental experience, an approach for which
there is no substitute if theology is to stand firm before the questioning of modern man as to whether all this talk about the
divinization of man, the sonship of God, the indwelling of God
is not simply poetry and undemonstrable mythology. Let me
emphasize once again that such a transcendental approach to
the theology of grace implies a transcendental approach to the
whole of theology. Especially since today ontic Christology,
despite its enduring worth, ungently needs translation into an

onto-logical Christology, that is, a Christology which from the very beginning understands the nature to be assumed by the Son of God not as a thing but as transcendental personality, so that his substantial unity with the Logos can, in principle, be expressed with the concepts of self-possession and transcendence, since in this case the being and nature in question does not simply have, but *is,* self-possession and transcendence. If that which is meant by the hypostatic union is to be clearly and sufficiently protected from the accusation of mythology, then it must be translated into these concepts. The whole of theology needs this approach of transcendental anthropology because the whole of theology is determined by the doctrines of Trinity, grace, and incarnation which mutually condition one another, and these three basic doctrines of Christianity must be treated transcendentally, both because the present time requires it, and also as a matter of principle.

2. Now it would be possible to raise the objection against what has been said: if such a transcendental anthropology were really necessary as a method of approach for the whole of theology then it must always have existed, because there has always been good theology. However, since it is obviously not the case that it has always existed, the demand cannot be legitimate. In reply to this it must be pointed out that there is an essential difference between preaching and theology, even though preaching in the concrete always does have an element of theological reflection in it and theology in the concrete never exhausts the Church's proclamation *(Verkündigung)* (even today theological eschatology, for example, is almost entirely still in the pre-theological stage of proclamation, and even the ecclesiology of Vatican II is to a large extent little more than a systematic arrangement of biblical images, except perhaps for some sections concerned with the legal structure of the Church). From this point of view, it is by no means a priori impossible that a genuinely scientific theology, that is, one carried out in

transcendental reflection, may not yet exist in many respects. Why should that not be possible? The fact that a great deal has been thought, discussed, and written in theology and systematized in some fashion or other, and that this is good and praiseworthy, is still no proof that that stage of reflection and conceptuality has been reached which can effectively distinguish theology from proclamation. But this stage has really been reached where and insofar as reflection is expressly carried on transcendentally, that is, where the a priori conditions for the knowledge of a particular object of faith are explicitly reckoned with, and where the concepts used to describe these theological objects are determined by this reflection.

In addition I am, of course, by no means maintaining that this method of transcendental anthropology has been entirely lacking in theology up till now. There can be no question about this. There is no time now to show with examples that this transcendental method, even if it has not been carried out explicitly and in principle, nevertheless, at the very least since Thomas, has been at work everywhere in theology, if admittedly with varying intensity. Finally, however, no matter what may be the situation with this historical question, it must be said that today the method of transcendental anthropology is demanded by the situation of the times. Plato, Aristotle, Thomas will alway remain living philosophers, from whom we must learn. That, however, does not change the fact (even if Catholic philosophy has begun to take notice of it only over the last forty years) that philosophy and, therefore, theology today cannot and must not go back to the time before the transcendental anthropology of modern philosophy, to the time before Descartes, Kant, German Idealism, and the philosophy of existence. This whole modern philosophy, if you will, is deeply unchristian, insofar as it carries on a transcendental philosophy of the autonomous personal subject (with few exceptions, such as Blondel), an autonomous personal subject which has closed itself to transcendental experience. But this philosophy is also most deeply Christian, (more than its traditional critics in the scholastic philosophy of modern times have understood) because in the Christian understanding man is not one element in a cosmos of things, subject to a coordinate-system of ontic concepts constructed from things. Man is the personal subject from whose freedom as a subject the fate of the entire cosmos depends. Otherwise, the history of salvation or damnation could have no cosmological meaning. Otherwise a cosmology revolving around Christ would be a childish playing with words. This inner division, the *simul justus et peccator*, is not only a hallmark of modern philosophy, but of every human work, and hence of philosophy in every age. It ought not to prevent us from seeing what is Christian in the intellectual efforts and achievements of modern times. It should not prevent us from accepting this situation in its basic character as something which from now on cannot be dispensed with in a modern Christian philosophy and theology. Perhaps one could say that this modern age, for which this transcendental anthropology is particularly suited, is already past or is in decline, and therefore, this philosophy also with it. There may be an element of truth, or even much truth, in this, but philosophies do not change like fashions. Rather, they are assimilated into the new philosophy of a new historical epoch, and so they preserve that which is most characteristic of them. If Christian neoscholastic philosophy, and with it theology, have slept through the modern era, they cannot be considered relieved of the task which modern philosophy posed for them simply because this philosophy in its present form may happen to be in decline. The ground must still be covered, if theology is to do justice to the period which comes after the modern era. This is especially true because what will presumably be tomorrow's philosophy, one corresponding to the increased realization of the social which will characterize tomorrow, will have its roots in German Idealism, perhaps in the Hegelianism of the left and its critique of ideologies, etc. If the themes of this philosophy of tomorrow are going to be hope, society, critique of ideology, a new form of freedom in a new social structure, the experience of God in the experience of man planning himself and his own future, then man becomes once again the indispensable subject matter of philosophy. And so, even from the point of view of the philosophy of tomorrow, the application of a transcendental anthropology is demanded of the theology of today and of tomorrow.

3. Finally, the need for theology to be transcendental anthropology can be established in a third way, that is, from the point of view of fundamental theology and apologetics. The trend in Protestant theology, and even outside it, towards "demythologization" is rooted in a serious concern; it aims, despite much that is precipitate, heretical, and unacceptable, at a kind of theology that we must have in the future, but which does not yet exist to a sufficient degree, if the ancient and enduring gospel is to be preached credibly. One can say, and with some justification, that the theology of demythologization is a new edition of the old liberalism and rationalism. This may well be. But have we sufficiently appreciated the genuine concerns and problems which gave rise to this rationalistic liberal theology? This is still the question.

Orthodox Protestant theology and Catholic theology as well have comforted themselves too readily with the thought that the school of Barth has routed the old liberal school in Protestant theology. Granted that a great deal of Barth and his achievements will remain, the fact is that Bultmann has really won the day over Barth in European Protestant theology as a whole. And this is not just a cruel and unjust accident in the history of ideas. To modern man there are thousands of theological propositions which savor of mythology, and which he does not consider himself seriously able to believe any longer. In the last analysis his attitude is, of

course, wrong. But there are real causes for his impression. And
these are to be found not solely in his personal pride and stu-
pidity, nor in the mysterious character of the truths and realities
of faith. This is especially true if we think of theological expressions according to the way they reach the ear of the average man
today and the way in which they are almost inevitably understood by him. Let us look honestly at the intellectual situation
of today. When a man who has not been educated as a Christian
hears the statement, Jesus is God made man, his first reaction
will be to reject this statement as a myth, which he cannot
possibly take seriously and which is not even worth discussing,
just as we do when we hear that the Dali Lama regards himself
as a reincarnation of Buddha. He hears of two people, similar
in personal qualities and attitudes, who are dying. On being told
that one goes straight to heaven because he happens to receive a
papal indulgence at the hour of death, while the other will spend
many years in purgatory because the pope as bearer of the keys
of heaven has not opened its gates to him, then this non-Christian will regard indulgences, *explained in this way,* as a clerical
invention, against which his idea of God protests violently. Nor
will he be easily convinced that God desires the salvation of all
men, even children before they have reached the age of reason,
and even after the fall, but yet that he cannot allow children
dying without baptism to his vision because he cannot get
around his own law about the necessity of baptism. Examples
could be multiplied. I cannot overcome the impression that
theology has not yet coped sufficiently with all these innumerable
difficulties, especially with regard to the successful teaching of
religion.

Again, from the point of view of apologetics, there is not
much value in appealing to the fact that it is a *mystery* which
God has revealed. If the fact of revelation were psychologically
so compelling and so clear that doubt was not possible, then
its content could be imposed positivistically as a mystery not to

be discussed. But if through the fault of theology modern man finds the content of revelation incredible, then, not entirely without logic, he will consider himself justified in doubting even more strongly the fact of revelation. This observation shows, incidentally, that we must strive for a much greater synthesis or union between fundamental and dogmatic theology than we have at present.

I believe that all the difficulties which men of today experience have a common basis: theological expressions are not formulated in such a way that they can see how what is being said has any connection with their own understanding of themselves, which they have derived from their experience. It cannot be required, and it would be heretical modernism if one attempted to deduce all theological propositions from this experience which man has of himself. That is not what is meant here, although this problem is more difficult than the traditional foes of modernism, for the most part, believe—for example, if one remembers that there is also such a thing as an experience of grace and that this grace is the chief and fundamental reality of Christianity itself. But if we prescind from this question here, still the connection between man's experience of himself and the content of dogmatic propositions can be looked upon otherwise than as simple logical deduction or explication.

There is a connection by correspondence, and especially there is a connection by the fact that "nature," understood as personal and transcendent, is an inner constitutive and necessary element, not indeed of grace as such in the abstract, but in the reality and the process in which grace is actually given. If such connections were discovered and reflected on, and especially if they were considered as being required by the content of the dogmatic statements, rightly understood, then not only would these propositions appear more credible from the catechetical point of view: the working out of these connections would enable us to penetrate the sense of these statements much more deeply, to avoid possible misunderstandings, unsuitable modes of representation, and unjustifiable conclusions. The discovery of such connections between the content of dogmatic statements and man's experience of himself is, however, in fact, nothing other than the obverse side of a transcendental anthropological method in theology. Therefore, this is necessary for reasons arising from fundamental theology and apologetics.

III.

What consequences would follow for theology if these needs for a transcendental anthropology were met? We shall answer this question by way of conclusion with a few examples. Above all, this method would, for the first time, enable us to give a credible account of the process of revelation in the bearer of revelation himself. It is odd how little our customary fundamental theology is able to give a clear picture of the process by which revelation takes place in the prophet himself, so that it does not appear simply as an unintelligible "miracle" (*Mirakel, anstatt als Wunder*), or to explain why this process shows so many parallels to analogous phenomena in the history of religion. The methods suggested here could be very fruitful for arriving at certain insights. We could conceive of man, for example, by this method of transcendental deduction, as the being who listens to God in history. We could come to realize and understand the fact that the word of God can exist only insofar as it is heard and believed and yet still remain the word of *God*. From there we might investigate how man is constituted in his being as hearer of the word of God through the grace of God which is God's gift of himself to man; and from there we might arrive at the realization that the history of salvation, which is grace, and the transcendental history of revelation are coextensive, and that the latter is not identical with *official* history of revelation as known a posteriori from historiography and

confined to a particular geographical locality (even if in addition
one postulates the existence of a "primitive revelation").

All these problems imply a transcendental inquiry. A correct
understanding of the nature of miracles (*des Wunders, samt
Abgrenzung von Mirakel*) could be promoted if the question
were raised by this transcendental method, why man, by his very
being, must reckon with such a thing as miracles, and therefore
why true miracles from the outset can only have a place within
a context where it is a question of the salvation of the whole
man. If there is such a thing as a history of salvation, which
itself is necessary for salvation, then theology must treat the
topic of the *a priori* transcendental salvation—historicality of
man—just as history calls for a philosophy of historicality (and
this philosophy is even an element of that history). Up till now,
however, in scholastic theology there is scarcely anything which
can be called a theology of the salvation-historicality of man.
The history of salvation is narrated, but there is very little reflection on its formal structures and especially on its transcendental necessity. The significance of this method for the doctrine
of the Trinity and of Christology was touched on earlier and
does not need to be gone into further here.

Because a theology of salvation history and of the transcendental salvation-historicality of man is lacking for the most part,
many prerequisites for an adequate ecclesiology are also lacking.
The foundation of the Church in her formal authority and
structure is usually treated in such a way that God could have
founded such a Church, if he had wanted to, at any time. The
place of the Church in eschatology and the history of salvation,
which is quite vital for her whole being, is scarcely considered
in our normal ecclesiology. Understanding for such an eschatological phase of salvation history is lacking however because
transcendental reflection on salvation-historicality and on the
phases of salvation history which are conditioned by this historicality has been lacking. But then how can we make the claim

credible that there is now an infallible Pope, when mankind and God, in their common care for the salvation of all men, had to, and did, get along without such an infallible source of truth for perhaps two million years? Changes in history which are important for salvation only become credible if it is expressly shown that man, by his very being, must have a history of his salvation. Therefore, even with regard to his salvation, it is not just a question of the eternally structured values of his being as such, but that even here man must rely on concrete history with its successive phases. With such an approach, the true nature of the Church's infallibility could probably also be more clearly distinguished from the negative aspects which unavoidably accompany it as they do all human reality. We need not explain further why a good ecclesiology has need of all those concepts which we derive only from a transcendental analysis of the nature and necessity of human intercommunication.

The method which we have suggested has a wide and important field of application also in the theological treatment of the sacraments. What other way have we of elaborating in a fitting way the nature of symbols, of the capacity and need which man has for symbols, of the fundamental concept of symbolic causality, and of the function of the symbol in human intercommunication? All these are important presuppositions for the doctrine of the sacraments and its correct understanding. If it were clear that grace is not a thing but has onto-logical character, that it is the condition for personal acts towards the immediacy of God, which itself is the gift of God, then it would be seen much clearer than it usually is that the baptism of infants should not be taken as the basic model of a sacrament. A sacrament would be understood as the transmission by means of a historical, inter-personal symbol of God's permanent offer of himself to the free human individual at the decisive moments of his life: an offer directed to the transcendental being of man. If we understood this, we should be in no danger of confusing the sacraments with magic. We would then be able to formulate comprehensible principles for the frequency of receiving the sacraments, and the sevenfold number of the sacraments could be more easily explained, a thing which it is by no means easy to do if one proceeds in purely positivistic, historical manner. Then it would be much clearer, e.g., that the effect of an indulgence cannot be conceived in any other way than as a deepening and intensification of love, gradually enfolding the whole being of man.

The major part of moral theology, if we prescind from faith, hope, and charity, on the one hand, and from positive ecclesiastical laws, has to do with what we are accustomed to call "natural law," and, indeed, it must. Quite apart, therefore, from the question of how we can define the relationship between this natural law and grace, we must realize that, in any case, a satisfactory justification of such a "natural law" is only possible by a transcendental deduction of the nature of man and, in addition, of his fundamental involvement in an historical situation which places him under a moral obligation. We shall not understand it, however, through any merely a posteriori collection of factual characteristics or peculiarities of man's individual or social existence, even when these occur quite generally. For not everything that is, not even everything which is generally true or appears to be, is therefore something that has to be. It is precisely in moral theology that the use of transcendental anthropology could obtain insights which would be of considerable practical importance, especially (not only!) with regard to the discrediting of claims which have been set up unjustifiably as based on natural law.

An eschatology which would measure up to modern demands needs as a basis a transcendental anthropology, in which man appears as that being who projects himself towards the expanding future, as the being characterized by hope and which has been made capable of an absolute future by God. Only in the light of such a futurology which has a transcendental and anthropocentric form can we discover those hermeneutical principles for the interpretation of eschatological statements. These principles are needed today if the statements themselves are to appear credible. It seems to me that scholastic eschatology is still not far from the mentality of the professor of dogmatic theology who declared that he had never maintained that the last trumpet of the archangel Michael was a material trumpet, but that he nevertheless defended stoutly the proposition that its tone was a material tone. Instead of developing a real theology, which involves a critical interpretation of literary imagery, scholastic eschatology has contented itself with producing a kind of jigsaw puzzle which aims at fitting together the images of the bible in one global picture, yet these images can never be brought together into any coherent picture, nor were they ever intended to be so brought together. A transcendental basis for the treatment of the last things would make it clear that eschatology does not aim to be some sort of anticipatory account given us by God (who actually sees them already) of what future events will actually look like. Rather such an eschatology would be seen as the necessary interpretation of man's *present* eschatological existence, from the viewpoint of his absolute future—an interpretation which belongs to the very being of man.

NOTES

1 The word "horizon" is used here not in the usual English sense of something which we may widen or expand or go beyond, but in the Heideggerian sense of a frame-work or viewpoint which provides the limits for certain activities performed within it (cf. M. Heidegger, *Being and Time*, Eng. translation by Macquarrie and Robinson, p. 19, note 4).

HENRI DE LUBAC

Nature and Grace

A Council need not speak of everything. Even what it does speak about need not be based on theological theories worked out beforehand and tested for rational coherence. It does not seek, it does not argue: it teaches, it declares the faith. Even when it does not pronounce a definition and even when it expresses views which do not all touch the mystery of the faith, its teachings constitute for us major premises rather than conclusions. Hence there enters into the exercise of the *magisterium* a prophetic element. It is the theologian's task to discern this element, to seize on it, so to speak, in order to submit his mind to it, and then subsequently work with it, with a view to a better under-standing of the faith.

The pastoral Constitution on the *Church in the Modern World* is no exception to this general rule. In the years to come it will inspire more than one attempt at a theory which will justify rationally what it has to say regarding the relationships between the Church and the world. The principles which it sets forth, especially in the first part, will stimulate theological reflection. No doubt this will accelerate the development of that "Christian anthropology" so much needed in our times.

Hence, it is not in order to make up for some defect on the part of the Council to explain what it should have said and did not, but rather with a sense of following in the wake of the Council, and of accepting it in "the obedience of faith" that we have to take up certain problems today in order to give an account both of its teachings and of the temper of mind that it urges upon us. It is a question here then, if you wish, of an essay in prospective theology—entirely prospective, in the sense that I do not pretend to bring forward a ready-made theory, or even propose a definitive conclusion, but simply to point to a direction for research. But from another viewpoint it will be retrospective theology, because nothing solid can be achieved in theology without tested materials. All research must be first of all a recapture, through tradition. All renewal supposes continuity. This is a perennial truth, one which it could be convenient to term banal, but perhaps it is opportune to recall it. In short, I shall only suggest a certain number of ideas, ancient or modern, without putting forth anything truly novel.

I

I have spoken of Christian anthropology. This phrase best sums up the principle object of our Constitution. For the first part tells us what man is, individual and social, according to the Christian faith. It does so in order to draw from this description "the rule of human activity" expounded in the second part. Note that the purpose of this double description is not something general and outside of time. The Christian idea of man together with the rule of action consequent upon it are both confronted with the contemporary world in the midst of which the Christian must act.

But, through a large part of its population and of its intellectual elite, the contemporary world opposes to our faith a radically different conception of man, from which all consideration of God is banished, under a number of diverse forms. Denial of God: that is the common factor in many viewpoints and attitudes that the Christian today meets on all sides. Hence the paragraph on atheism has been rightly considered the *punctum saliens* of the whole Constitution.

This means that the main doctrinal task to which the Constitution *Gaudium et Spes* summons and stimulates us is a confrontation with contemporary atheism. I say rightly: confrontation. And yet I am not unmindful that the spirit urged upon us by this text, as by the whole work of the Council, is one of *dialogue* and of *comprehension*. The Holy Father's Encyclical *Ecclesiam suam* asks as much of us, and he spoke to the same effect in his address closing the Council last December 7:

"Anticlerical and profane humanism appeared in frightening proportions, and, in a manner, defied the Council. The religion of the God Who became man met the religion of man who makes himself God, if such be a religion. What happened? A collision, a struggle, an anathema? That could have happened but it did not. The ancient parable of the Good Samaritan furnished the model for the spirituality of the Council. A feeling of boundless sympathy coursed through it from beginning to end. The uncovering of human needs, which grow ever greater as the sons of earth mature, absorbed the attention of our synod. . . ."

In other words we Christians want to show by a sort of peaceful competition, in deeds as well as words, that "we also, we Christians, we, more than anyone else have the cult of man." And whatever be the type of atheism that the man before us represents, we accept him as a brother. We know that we have research to do in common with him. We force ourselves to understand him, to enter into his reasons, his difficulties, and even to understand his very incomprehensions, or his need of peace of mind, in order to speak to him, if possible, in such a way as to convince him.

The dialogue must be taken up not only with the atheist but also with atheism. So we must show ourselves capable of comprehending atheism itself. Here the meaning of these two words dialogue and comprehension takes on a different but not lesser importance. To the extent that we respect the man who speaks to us, and take his ideas seriously, dialogue once begun quickly becomes a confrontation: our part cannot consist in mere listening without response, nor in losing ourselves in the meanderings of an inconsistent relativism. Truth is one and, despite the subtleties invented more or less happily by fertile minds distrustful of a sharply-defined position, the stake of the dialogue is the inevitable reply to the question as to whether God exists or not. For clearing up naïve or distorted ideas of the faith or for pointing out to the other man the unfortunate ambiguity in certain of his apparent negations, it may be very useful to refer to the idea of "negative theology," or to suggest the mystical "nights" of a St. John of the Cross. But these must not be taken as a refuge from the urgency of the decision.

Therefore the dialogue is a confrontation and that amounts to admitting that it is a struggle. We need not fear admitting that we fight against atheism. As if struggle could be eliminated from life,—as if the life of a believer who runs into atheism could be other than a struggle for God! It is only a question of deciding how to fight, it is a question of what weapons to use. Since the warfare is spiritual, the weapons can only be spiritual, the weapons of light. And since such warfare must be fought simultaneously on two fronts, i.e., in the interior life and in exterior action, the spiritual weapons used will have no chance of being effective unless we use them at the same time against ourselves. It is only at this price that pharisaism is overcome; and it is only at this price that the struggle can be brought to a doubly happy issue against atheism, for the benefit of both the unbeliever and the believer. For the faith is no human value that we own like fixed capital, nor does it blend with other

values to make up our natural being, nor are we free to step out
of it for the sake of a more friendly approach to the man who
does not have it. It is an essentially living relation to a Reality
that rules us and judges us even while it enlightens us. It is a
Reality by which we live ever unworthily, even as regards the
understanding of it, and to which we are always more or less
unfaithful. Every situation is a chance to purify it, to strengthen
it and to deepen it, but none more so than the encounter with
atheism. No bending of the faith, even merely by way of method,
is going to help us to understand the fact of atheism better.
Rather the light of faith alone can light up this fact and uncover
its full meaning.

The contemporary world does not permit us to escape this
confrontation. Every believer must give this witness of faith. But
those whose office or competence implies intellectual reflection
are challenged to give an account in intellectual terms for the
faith of all their brethren.

They do this, first of all, by making an effort to *understand*.
The term "understanding" must be taken in a technical sense.
When two currents of thought confront each other, each strives
to understand the other. Anyway, such has been the strategy of
contemporary atheism. Scarcely anyone today would make a direct attack on the proofs of God's existence in order to refute
them by the methods of classical logic; nor would anyone deny
every shred of truth in the Christian mysteries. It is a question
rather of understanding and explaining them. A hermeneutic
is proposed which strives to go beneath the primary sense (which
alone exists for the simple believer in God's existence or the
divinity of Christ), in order to disclose a second meaning that is
more true, and which finally turns out to be the only true
meaning. And this second meaning is purely human. The at-
tributes of God are not necessarily denied, but as Feuerbach
said, they are transferred to their true owner. The death and
resurrection of Christ become sublime symbols of what is most

profound in man. Since historical processes must be gradual, unbelievers grant that belief in the primary sense of these mysteries was a necessary stage in the development of human consciousness. But today, it is proclaimed, times have changed. Just as the New Testament revealed the hidden meaning of the Old Testament, but by discarding it as old and as belonging to the dead past, so contemporary humanism does with its understanding of Christian theism. It believes that it understands it, does it justice, and raises it up into a second life within itself which is more true and is indeed the only truth. But by that very fact it relegates Christian theism in its first sense to the cemetery of myths. Should the thing of the past strive to survive or revive, it would then become an evil influence. The embrace that understands therefore grips in order to stifle.

Today such is the usual claim of atheism, the general form of its strategy, whether it be triumphant, despairing or placid; whether it inclines to collectivism or to anarchy; whether it derives from metaphysical renunciation, or from earthly ambition; or whether, in its totalitarian imperialism, it speaks in the name of sociology or psychoanalysis. So in order not to be "understood" in this sense, only one way is open: to do some understanding. Therefore the Christian must understand atheism. He must detect behind its deceptive hermeneutic the real sources from which it springs, their emptiness! He must suspect any mediocre and superficial "comprehension" based on desire of conciliation, since that will leave him defeated before he begins. He should be especially alert to reject the compromise formulas easily accepted unconsciously or half-consciously, that this atheistic hermeneutic puts out as bait, since through them he may slip into apostasy. Against the explanation which attempts to show him how "the religion of God made man leads by inevitable dialectic to an anthropology" and how it "was the symbolic expression of the social and human process" which alone is real, he must be able to bring forth a more penetrating explanation. His counter arguments should show that a rightly conceived anthropology supposes a theology, to which it leads by an inevitable dialectic: and he must show that the human social process finds its meaning and fulfillment not in man but in Jesus Christ the God-man. And he must show how "the religion of the Father" must remain in order that the Father might be "entirely with us," and that He should not be absorbed into us, thus leaving us quite by ourselves. Let him not hesitate to say that the absence of God is the misery of man, and let him proclaim his faith as the interior power that restores his dignity to man, and hope to the world.

Such is the first task imposed upon us by the Constitution *Gaudium et Spes*. It is so fundamental and boundless that this paper can do no more than point it out.

II

Let us now reconsider our Constitution and notice the connection of its two parts. At first sight the second part appears to be an application to particular problems of general principles set forth in the first part. This is not false and it can be argued from the transitional paragraph at the beginning of the second part. But the mutual relation of the two parts can also be understood otherwise. The title of the first part is somewhat ambiguous, and doubtless this ambiguity was necessary to permit the entire subject matter to be covered: "The Church and Human Vocation." Human vocation means the calling of man; and the whole subsequent treatment shows that this calling is not merely human, but divine. Man created in the image of God is called to eternal life, in God; and thus each of the four chapters, following a sort of indirect ascending route, culminates in the recall of the Lord's return and of the kingdom to come. By contrast, the second part, setting out from Christian principles and with their help, redescends to questions of the temporal order, and it takes these up from their most contemporary garb in order to find proper solutions.

Hence the two parts of the Constitution give rise to two great problems, connected but opposite, which will invite theological investigation during the years to come. Theologians should seek where possible rational justifications for the teachings that the Council, following its role, has promulgated as simple statements, by an act of authority.

On the one hand, beginning with man, it will be a question of establishing his obligation to move, in the liberty of his personal life, towards that divine destiny which Jesus Christ allots and promises him through the Church. On the other hand, supposing the first problem solved, the reverse perspective demands that we establish the Christian's attachment to the realities of this world, and the duty imposed on him to work for the temporal development of mankind in every field. Evidently the two problems crisscross. But for the theologian the tasks are very different. Seen in their logical outline, the first is a problem of convincing the unbeliever that he ought to be prepared to listen to the Good News; the second is to try to convince the believer of the legitimate value of the things of earth and time, precisely from the point of view of that supernatural order into which God has introduced him, and of that eternal life to which he aspires. Indeed the second argument must go further and prove too that the Christian vocation is ultimately the only satisfying motive for the struggle to promote natural progress. However, in fact, the mind does not move in such straight lines. Abstractly considered the two problems may be distinct and run in opposite direction, but in fact they constantly interfere and overlap with each other, and it is only for the sake of clarity that, by a process of simplification, we treat them separately.

The first of these two problems did not arise yesterday. According to difference of time and place, and under different aspects, the problem has ever been that of understanding the

relation that holds between two basic elements which theological tradition has canonized under the names of (human) nature
and the supernatural.

In the last few centuries, a theory gained acceptance according
to which nature and supernature each constituted a complete
order. The second of these was so added to the first that no
other tie remained between them than that the natural order
had a vague and general "obediential potency" to be "elevated,"
according to the terminology of the theory. The dualistic character of this conception need not be emphasized, since it is well
known to all theologians. It seemed necessary to guarantee the
absolute gratuity of the divine gift against a succession of
serious errors that began with laicism of the 16th century and
continued up to the modernist immanentism of the 20th century.
In fact, its presuppositions derived from a rupture of the traditional dogmatic synthesis, such as had been elaborated finally by
the great scholastics, and particularly by St. Thomas Aquinas.
Its disadvantages are quite apparent and have often been de-
nounced. The supernatural gift henceforth appeared as a super-
imposed reality, as an artificial and arbitrary superstructure. The
unbeliever found it easy to withdraw into his indifference in
the very name of what theology was telling him: if my very
nature as a man truly has its end in itself, what should oblige
or even arouse me to scrutinize history in the quest for some
other vocation perhaps to be found there? Why should I listen
to a Church which bears a message having no relation to the
aspirations of my nature? Should not the intrusion of some outside supernatural even be rejected as a kind of violence?

During the last eighty years the situation has greatly changed
in this regard. Gradually and under the influence of different
factors, the majority of theologians have returned to more traditional views, while attempting to update their modes of expression. But at the very time when this dualism was being rejected
in theological schools, here and there it was achieving new
fortune in the domain of practical action.

While theologians were striving to protect the supernatural from all contamination, it became isolated from the life of the mind, and from social life, and the field was left clear for the invasion of secularism. Today this secularism, ever advancing, is trying to invade the conscience of Christians themselves. General agreement is sometimes sought on the basis of an idea of nature that would be acceptable both to the theist and to the atheist. Whatever comes from Christ or would lead to Him is then relegated to the shadows,—"to a retired center" of the mind,—where it may well disappear forever. The climax of Christian progress and of entering into adult age would then seem to consist in a total "secularization" that would banish God not only from social life but from culture and even from the relationships of private life. Henceforth no more conflicts are possible, no more tragedies need be feared, no more tensions need appear in the bosom of our society through division on the question as to the ultimate meaning of life. It suffices to distinguish adequately on the one hand "the human hopes" that put into effect an entirely human idea of man, and on the other hand "supernatural hope."

The Christian could rally without scruples to the first hopes respecting the natural and earthly man, while he kept fast the second hopes in the depths of his heart. He could easily come to an understanding with the unbeliever about the estimation and development of "human values," while keeping clear "of the diversity of religious and philosophic options." For though man be destined to see God, and though the embrace of God ought to be "the crown of the human adventure," it should never be forgotten that this end is "wholly gratuitous." And in good logic the conclusion is that, "in the human reality, in the existing historical conditions," the recognition of "the religious dimension" is not at all necessary "to human fulfillment." "An atheistic attitude" is entirely legitimate. The thesis must be pushed further; it must be recognized fearlessly that this attitude is the only legitimate one: "grace is no solution to the enigma of

life, nor is it a rival to the creative autonomy of man." Any
desire to make it interfere for any reason whatsoever "in the
interworldly dynamism of human evolution," would be to make
it "an element of alienation," and to cause it to be accursed as
"an intruder threatening to eclipse (cast a shadow on) the ethical
splendor of Prometheus."

The solution is simple. But it holds cheap (thinks little of) that
unity which, embracing distinctions and even the deepest con-
trarieties, ought to be the hallmark of all human thought and
life worthy of the name. It is easy; but since it shuts out the
gospel from life, it is partisan to every surrender—and itself is
already surrender. If this theory were true, the greater part of
the Constitution *Gaudium et Spes* would be to no purpose. Its
very foundation would be reduced to rubble. The Church could
tell us nothing about the things of this world, because the course
of human affairs could receive no light from the gospel. And
hence as the years to come will see the Church ever more en-
grossed in the problems raised in our Constitution, it will be
ever more incumbent on theology to dig into this fundamental
problem of the relationship of human nature to the supernatural
order.

Obviously, this involves theological research, a thing which presupposes faith, and is carried out under the light of faith. This
should not, however, be confused with that type of apologetics
which is intended to convince the man who as yet does not
believe, that first tried to get him to recognize a "natural desire"
in himself and then to believe that this natural desire should
lead him to the "supernatural word" revealed in Jesus Christ.
For the analysis of such a natural desire does not belong either
to mere psychological observation or to rational reflection left
to itself. As analysis penetrates certain types of human behavior,
it encounters something ambiguous whose meaning cannot be
had except by faith. At the same time that the God-man Jesus
Christ reveals God to us, He reveals us to ourselves. Without

God the ultimate recesses of our being remain an enigma. The situation here is similar to that of the proofs for the existence of God: they become obscure to the mind at the very moment when they are most needed. Similarly, in a climate of atheism, the teaching on "natural desire" lacks a necessary, presupposed common idea of "nature." Christian thought should be at the very least coherent not only for the intellectual satisfaction of the believer, but because his witness to the world demands it. And in the face of any appearances to the contrary whatsoever, we must maintain our trust in man and in the message that we have received from Christ. For we know that the two are made for each other. Recalling to man his final end is not telling him something that is of no fundamental interest to him, despite the obstacles that here and now prevent him from recognizing it. Rather it is helping him to find and then decipher the inscription engraved in him by his Creator. It is snatching him away from anguish, despair and unfortunate illusions. It exalts his stature: *"Celsa creatura, in capacitate Majestatis"* (St. Bernard). For man's end is so sublime that he needs God in order to obtain it, but thereby, *"non vilificatur, sed dignificatur"* (Scotus). We do not claim that such truths as these will find easy acceptance. But they are vastly more meaningful and powerful than a more timid position based on the aforesaid dualism which restricts itself to the so-called truths of the natural order.

III

We have already somewhat crossed over into the territory where the second problem occurs. In the nature of the case, the two problems cannot be entirely separated. We have already said that the phrase "the human vocation" in the title of the first part of *Gaudium et Spes* contains at the same time the Christian vocation of man and the human vocation of the Christian; it is a double vocation, embracing both time and eternity, both earth and heaven. And the second part of the Constitution tells us, by means of a number of examples, both how the eternal vocation has repercussions in the temporal order, and how temporal action in return has repercussions in eternity. Or rather, this second aspect is only lightly treated, and constitutes precisely the problem: How to justify the interest which the Church shows in this temporal action.

At the end of the Constitution the council Fathers say that they have committed themselves on many subjects, basing themselves on the Word of God and on the spirit of the gospel, in order to bring to all men, whether Christians or not, effective assistance towards the enormous work that man must accomplish: the building of the world in peace. The preceding discussion has shown that the light which revelation sheds on the temporal world has great value for it, or at least, has shown the direction in which we must go to see it. But now it is the reverse which is the problem: How is the building of the world a matter of concern for eternal life?

Let us consider briefly two things that have their importance, but which do not yet bring us to the heart of the problem.

The Christian knows, without having to look any further, that he must be faithful to the gospel, and consequently he considers that the practice of justice and charity must be the first of his duties. That is a program which has many and wide-ranging applications, which commits him to ever renewed efforts, and which will make him everywhere present in the affairs of this world. The Christian knows that the world was created by God and that a good God's creation is good. The world is worthy of wonder and love, it is worth the trouble involved in research and concern. And because man is an active being as well as a contemplative, he should put the world's great resources to their best possible use, not only for the necessities of life, but in order that by savoring the world's many flavors man himself may be brought to human fulfillment. Indeed the Christian knows that a house is being prepared for him in the next world; and that in his own nature there is some kind of flaw, which forces him to distrust himself in the use of this world; he knows that he must not allow himself to be submerged by it. But that does not abolish the basic goodness of creation. Our fundamental attitude towards the world and to man's great efforts to put it to the best human use must be positive, and such is the attitude of our Constitution.

The Church could have restricted herself to the first of these two considerations and still fulfilled her central duty. If, on the contrary, she had treated only the second, she would have neglected her own mission. But in the second part of *Gaudium et Spes*, she takes two more steps, and this leads us to recognize a twofold problem. She affirms, or rather she constantly presupposes, a certain correspondence between the goodness of things belonging to the natural order (and this includes the achievements of culture and civilization), the goodness of human and earthly realities, and the divine, supernatural destiny to which each man is called in the mystery of Christ. Moreover, adopting a perspective which is habitually collective and dynamic, she takes for granted, or at least appears to take for granted, the idea of a future progress of mankind, a progress which itself must be put in some relationship to man's supernatural destiny.

Of two problems which thus thrust themselves upon theological reflection, the first has already been solved in principle by traditional theology. *Gratia supponit naturam:* one needs but liberate the thousand concrete applications that this thomistic principle contains. The more a man is a man, rich in humanity, either by qualities inborn, or by his culture, the more grace will find in him privileged terrain in which it can accomplish its task. No doubt the caprices of the subjective life must not be discounted. It is well known that a fortunate balance of natural gifts can favor a merely human ideal of wisdom that constitutes a block to the entry of the spirit of God. Peguy's well-known epigram comes to mind to the effect that some people are too moral for the waters of grace to get them wet. But objectively speaking, and all other things being equal, it must be conceded that greater mental lucidity and a stronger will allow a freer and more thoroughgoing commitment in man's reply to God's call. "Is it not evident that, however transcendent be the love and zeal of God, they cannot come except to a heart that is *human;* that is to say, a heart prepared (remotely or proximately) by all the juices of the earth?" For example, "who can say how much our most supernatural mystical life owes to a Plato, a Leibniz, a Pascal, a Newton and to many others, even more unexpected, that each of us could name in his heart?" The order of charity raises and transfigures whatever is human, but it draws its materials from the human. A St. Gregory of Nyssa has taken note of this fact, and has shown the positive if preparatory role to be assigned to natural "passion" in the development of the spiritual life. Without this passion, said he, "what in the world could motivate us to seek after heavenly things?"

And for this very reason material and technical progress are not without interest for the supernatural order, if it is true that they have repercussions on the progress of the human conscience. At the very least this points to matter for future research. And here we come before a truly novel problem that is set before the theologian by the Constitution *Gaudium et Spes.* For this progress of conscience that correlates with technical progress is not a question of the life of the individual, but rather of that of the entire human species.

The Constitution takes for granted that such progress of mankind is a fact, and that this progress concerns the kingdom of God. Such a state of affairs is asserted and re-asserted, but the task of explaining it is left to us. A due distinction is made between "earthly progress" and "the growth of the kingdom of Christ"; but along with this the first is declared to have great importance for the second, because it can "contribute to a better organization of human society" and thus constitutes "a certain foreshadowing of the world to come." Before being "transformed" the cosmos must be brought to its "fulfillment" (#39). The assertions are plain enough, but the indications are vague as to the direction future thought must take. The problems are huge, and a little reflection shows they branch out in every direction.

There was a man of our time who set himself to unravel these things. That man was not a professional theologian; his insights were too partial and often not too sure. Yet, perhaps it is not rash to find a certain indirect and diffused influence of his in some of the attitudes of the Council. That man was Father Teilhard de Chardin. As regards our question, Father Teilhard must be credited with making the problem of the end of the world an actual problem for us. Guided by faith, his meditation culminates in "an expectancy of the Parousia," "that unique and supreme event wherein the historical is joined to the Transcendent." But according to him the human effort to promote technical, social and even mental progress (an effort which takes place as the result of a process which largely escapes the liberty of the individual), will bring about the natural conditions of maturation that will make possible the Return of the Lord. These conditions are necessary, but of course they are "not sufficient"! To explain his position, he points to the first coming of Christ. The Incarnation had to be prepared for by the whole history of Israel. And that history presupposed long and complex developments preceding it. And so St. Paul could affirm that the coming of Christ was in the fullness of time. But the Incarnation was not for all that less gratuitous, free and transcendent with respect to all that had prepared it. And such, concludes Teilhard, must be the case with the Second Coming. Human development will be a necessary but not sufficient condition of its occurrence.

It seems that none of that could be challenged in the name

of Christian faith. But how many questions spring up before us!
Questions about the fact of this human development, and about
its nature; questions about the role assigned to technical
progress in the progress of conscience; questions about the rami-
fications of this dynamic conception of the world in the field of
morals; questions about the relation of this collective eschatology
to individual eschatology; questions about the necessity of natural conditions for the supernatural event of the Parousia; questions about the comparative role of human development and of
Christian hope in the preparation for and the coming of the
last day, etc., etc. We have no intention of taking up the
particularities of the teilhardian system; this does not belong
to our subject. Just about the same questions come to the fore
out of the text of the conciliar Constitution. At any rate the
Constitution leaves these questions open.

Some other important questions suggest themselves. How is
it possible to understand the final integration of this temporal
world into the eternal kingdom? How should the integration of
nature into the supernatural be understood? How can one set
forth the rhythm that ought to regulate this integration, so as
to reproduce the rhythm of the mystery of Christ, which is a
mystery of incarnation, death and resurrection? Has tradition
some light, so far neglected, to shed on this subject? In the years
to come how should one go about following up *Gaudium et Spes*
with a more explicit and rigorous Eschatology? Finally—and this
is essentially the same problem,—how can we complete the
Council's moral teachings with those mystical vistas that are indispensable for the consummation of the faith?

E. SCHILLEBEECKX

Faith Functioning in Human Self-Understanding

In our days the unsettled account of the modernistic and anti-modernistic tumult still lies open in front of us. A conclusive answer to the real problematic of Modernism was never given; the problem was only covered up. Ultimately the position taken by the ecclesiastical hierarchy in opposition to Modernism was only, and rightly, to block the ways which in no event would lead to a solution. But theologians opposed Modernism with elaborate scholastic viewpoints which answered to an altogether different problem and passed over the new question. The vehement anti-modernistic reaction had as a result that for a long time no one even dared to consider the problem. The whole problematic had begun with, let us say, Schleiermacher—not to speak of Feuerbach. It was developed further, in another manner, by Modernism. Since then, the problem has been more clearly and radically posed in various forms by Bultmann, Ebeling, P. Tillich, H. Braun, Th. Altizer, J. Robinson, P. van Buren, and H. Cox, though with various distinctions among themselves. This whole question has yet to find a conclusive answer on the Catholic side. Catholic theologians have, on the whole, avoided the problem, with the result that the question of the re-interpretation of dogma is now spreading unrest in Catho-

lic circles. This is because we have been accustomed to view the
understanding of truth in a purely conceptualistic way.

It is not my intention to analyze the essence of this question,
nor to examine how the premises of the whole problem are
already found in the Enlightenment and in the reformation
thought of the nineteenth century. I only want to clear the
field and draw a few basic lines and boundaries within which
Catholic thought can open up new perspectives.

I. MAN HIMSELF IS A RELIGIOUS QUEST

Through God's absolute and gratuitous self-communication to
man, man comes to a new, reborn relationship with God. Thus,
grace is, as an interpersonal communion with God, an undeserved yet real qualification of man's being. This implies that
revelation and grace presuppose the human person as condition
for their own possibility. The theological concept "nature," as
distinguished from "supernature," does not refer to the Aristotelian category, but is an intrinsic implication of revelation itself. The free acceptance of revelation would be intrinsically
meaningless, if this revelation did not presuppose a responsive
subject as the condition of its own possibility. This subject can
then accept and in his own personal life meaningfully assimi-
late the salvation which is offered to him as a free gift of God.
God wants to give himself, wants to be freely and personally
accepted by man. This means that we can say just as well "gratia
supponit naturam," and "natura supponit gratiam."

In view of the foregoing problematic, we can consider three
aspects of that "nature," seen theologically, that is, the condition
presupposed in and by grace itself as prerequisite for its very
possibility.

1) *Human self-understanding, as the intrinsic condition for
the possibility of revelation, and thus as inner dimension
of the faith.*

The human person is the subject presupposed in and by grace itself. However, this human person is not an enclosed inner reality which, already complete in itself, is subsequently incarnated in the world through a body. It is essentially a spirit-in-the-world, indeed spirit or person, but in self-communication to a physical body which is thereby humanized and to a certain extent, and with various gradations, "subjectivized." Precisely because man is no pure self, no pure spirit, but a spirit that must actuate itself in a body, he becomes present to himself only while going out of himself. The human self is essentially in and with the objects of this world. Thus, man sees his inner reality only when he looks out on the world of men and objects, consequently, only in association with men in the world. He is only present to himself, only person, when he is with something else, and especially with another person. Self-consciousness is then the awareness of a self-that-is-in-the-world, a consciousness of being with other things and primarily with one's fellowmen. Psychology and phenomenology have made it clear that a man becomes acquainted with the world through knowing his fellowmen. In other words, the relation to one's fellowmen is in a certain respect primary in comparison with one's relation to the world. In a certain respect, I said: since being-in-the-world makes it possible for man as spirit in matter, expressing and revealing himself in bodiliness and worldliness, to direct himself toward the other, his fellowman. Consequently, man becomes present to himself only in a humanized world, that is to say, in a world which is, and insofar as it is, characterized by the signs of human presence. The self's being-in-the-world through self-revelation in matter is inescapably bound up with directing oneself to one's fellowman, and man becomes present to himself in confrontation with this double orientation.

"Nature," or the subject of grace, is thus concretely the human person who becomes present to himself in giving himself to another person. With respect to knowledge and consciousness, this means: human consciousness—the intrinsic condition for the possibility of revelation—is a self-awareness which is reached in and through the awareness of fellowmen in this world.

This self-awareness is present first and foremost in the manner of a pre-reflexive or unthematic self-understanding, previous to its being reflected upon. Before any reflection man experiences the existence which he and his fellows live out in this world. This pre-reflexive experience, however indistinct it is, is already a comprehending and clarifying perception, since one's conscious presence with fellow men in the world is: interpreting oneself in the world. Therefore, although human consciousness is initially indistinct and pre-reflexive, as self-awareness in and through the awareness of fellow men, it is already as self-understanding, a worldview and an ethical view of life, and all this at a definite moment of a history which is already filled with human meaning. Reflection, especially philosophy, does nothing else than continually clarify human existence in new situations. Consequently as presupposing the human subject, revelation, and thus faith in revelation, must imply man in this situation: as a being that searches for himself, a being that attempts to arrive at self-understanding. "Fides non potest universaliter praecedere intellectum: non enim posset homo assentire credendo aliquibus propositis, nisi ea aliqualiter intellegeret" (Sum. theol., II–II, q. 8, a. 8, ad 2).

2) *The world of human experience, the only access to revelation.*

In view of this anthropological structure of man, wherein bodiliness is the necessary point of reference for man's every personal activity—also therefore, and primarily, for his consciousness—or put another way: because perception is the basis of all human awareness, man's conscious presence with others in the world is his only access to explicit and actual knowledge of all other possible realities. In this sense man knows primarily

only the tangible world and, thus, everything that is related—
and insofar as it is related to this tangible world. That is to say,
in the first place, he knows himself and his fellowman, precisely
as being in the world. Subsequently, he knows God as creator of
this world; and—if this actually should occur—God as He manifests Himself in a unique and gracious way in this world.

This means that the world of human experience is the only
access to the saving reality of revelation and faith. For that
matter, how could we listen to a revelation from God—how can
it be a revelation to man, if it falls outside our experience? It
is impossible for man to know or be aware of realities which he
does not experience in some way or another.

3) *Human self-understanding and man's religious quest.*

If we consider the deepest meaning of man's being a creature,
then we have to say, in addition, that God himself belongs to
the full definition of man. This is so at least in the sense that
man, precisely in what he is as a being living through his own
bodiliness in a world of fellowmen and objects, is a transcendental relation to God. Transcendental relation: that is to say,
the very essence of the relative being is *itself* a relation. Inas-
much as his whole being is a participation of God, and just this
participation is what makes him a man, it follows that the pre-
reflexive self-consciousness of man, evoked in and through his
consciousness of the world and other men, is by its very nature
a religious self-consciousness. "Being present to oneself," the
very core of a knowing being—"cum ipsa anima naturaliter sit
sibi praesens" (*In I Sent.*, d.3, q.4, a.4)—means by its nature to
stand *before* God, however unexpressed that presence may be.
The self is a being which, in absolute relation to God, points
to and tends toward the world and other men, and as such is
present to itself.

Every human self-consciousness in and through the world is

therefore founded upon and constituted by an accompanying consciousness of God. We could therefore define man in this way: as a being-with-God-in-this-world-of-men-and-things. The humanizing of oneself in and through the humanizing of the world, together with other men, is thus anchored in the mystery of God, which is the foundation of everything. All this implies that the absolute and unique relation to God is the fundamental and co-conscious horizon of and in our manifold conscious relations to the world: this absolute relation enters into human self-consciousness in and through the relative relations to our fellowmen and the world. Consequently we cannot separate this absolute relation—to God—from our historically conditioned, inner-worldly relations to this world and to these fellowmen. Thus we cannot formalize this relation to God and abstract it out of the historical warp and woof of our existence. With respect to myself, God, the Transcendent, has no other ground than the contingency and gratuity of my historical existence. To eliminate my contingent existence in this world from my thinking would mean to eliminate the basis of my affirmation of the mystery of God, and thus to reason away the affirmation of God itself.

On the one hand, it is, of course, quite clear that, by definition, the absolutely transcendent God eludes any direct experience by man; if this were not the case, then, by definition, He would be a non-God. On the other hand, the affirmation of God's existence cannot be a logical conclusion from a premise which was first in itself "godless." From an atheistic premise we can never draw a theistic conclusion. If God exists, we can know this only through the mediation of the world of human experience, which is for us the only gate giving access to reality. It is not as though there were a particular and separate capacity in man, a special feeling for God, through which he could experience God in some particular way, apart from the general human experience of being. This experience of being is present in human self-consciousness, on the basis of man's living encounter with the world and fellow men. In this experience there is an implicit awareness of something which surpasses all human experience. Consequently, what is actually perceived is the dynamism of the experienced contingent reality in its objective reference toward the absolute constitutive mystery of God. The so-called "proof of God" is only the reflexive explicitation of this content of experience. Reality itself reveals itself to man as referring-back-to-God. The human spirit does no more than, in a projective act, as it were, follow in the footsteps of this objective dynamism as it is found in reality itself. In doing this, the spirit is carried along, not primarily by its own projection, but by the objective, ontic dynamism of the experienced reality, toward the personal existence of God as the mystery without which my world of experience would be intrinsically contradictory. The natural affirmation of God is therefore no more than a critically founded affirmation on the basis of human experience, that our life is secured in the personal mystery of God. Basing ourselves merely on this world, we cannot, of course, meet God in a genuine interpersonal relationship. But, because, by definition, mystery can only be possessed in surrender, man's interpretation of himself in human experience is the root of all religiosity, that is to say, is the human openness which can be raised by the graciousness of God to a God-centered, a "theologal" communion, with the living God.[1]

Man's relation of absolute dependence with respect to God permeates all his relations to the world and all his encounters with other men. His being, in all directions relational, also has a relational depth dimension, an absolute relationship, namely, the relation to God. Consequently, man is both absolutely and relatively relational, and indeed such that the absolute relation founds and constitutes all his relative relations. All this is present in the pre-reflexive human experience,[2] albeit in various grades (sometimes even in the form of refusal, whether of God, or of the world, or of fellow man). The nucleus of all human experience is: mystery as the horizon of awareness: a religious self-awareness in and through this historical world of men and things. Man is thus a being whose life at all its levels and in its whole historical existence has a religious depth dimension. All human interpretation and, thus, all man's relative relationships spring from an absolute relation which embraces all and is the foundation of all human significance. This basic, absolute relation does not in any sense provide us with *a priori* solutions to temporal problems, but it does urge us to seek solutions, and at the same time it gives us the guarantee that our search for relative meaning in this world is not itself meaningless, even though it gradually fades into mystery.

With these remarks we have no intention of creating something like the eighteenth century "natural religiosity;" nor do we want to abstract out of all existing religions a kind of general "religious *eidos*." The religious depth dimension of human experience takes shape only in the historical situations of our world and our fellowmen. It cannot be abstracted from this without destroying itself. To accept a kind of generally valid religious "minimum-substratum" on which all religions would be founded seems to me precisely a misunderstanding of the very structure of man. In man the religious dimension is only a depth dimension of the concrete, historical condition of his being situated in-the-world-with-fellowmen. This naturally implies that every concrete image of God functions with a determinate world-view. From human history, from every growing human history, the religious depth dimension of human consciousness takes its concrete shape.

However, this pre-reflexive religious self-awareness can never adequately be "gathered up" by the reflection: it continues to elude every reflexive human self-clarification. That is to say: human existence cannot be fully "X-rayed" by thinking; it cannot be wholly objectified. Thus man remains an absolute mystery for himself, that is, not simply a provisional mystery which, given time, might become fully clarified. The absolute mystery of God reverberates upon and flows into the very being of man, which, as participation of God, could only be fully explained if one could base oneself on the mystery of God. Therefore, man cannot adequately explain his own existence; he is withdrawn and hidden from himself. Reference to the absolute mystery of God belongs to the very being of man. Being present to oneself, self-awareness is therefore in the last analysis religious, is inescapably a religious act. Thus human existence does not leave man the choice to be *not*-religious: he is forced by his own being to be religious or irreligious, to love or to disavow his own being: and in both cases it is a question of a religiously relevant action. To stand before oneself is to stand before God.

But if it is established that a man becomes present to himself only in the giving of himself to his fellowmen, then we must conclude that this positive religious self-awareness concerns concretely and primarily the transcendental depth-dimension of human fellowship or of brotherly love. In the reality of actual life the pre-reflexive affirmation of God is the depth-dimension of every acceptance of one's fellowman. God is really that which makes possible our interhuman and worldly relationships. Hence these human relationships already have a relevant and meaningful relation to man's religious quest, positively or negatively.

Thus, "nature," as "subject of grace," means in fact: the human person, who by his very nature is an existential religious quest, because he is a creature, and cannot explain away the mystery of his own being. The "natural awareness of God"—expressed thematically in the so-called "proof of God"—and precisely as undeserved reality which can be approached in a humanly free way, that is, assented to or refused, for life or for death, is an intrinsic condition for the very possibility of revelation. The demand for abandonment to the mystery of reality is implied in the very nature of man's being. Consequently, the religious problematic cannot be evaded, at least in the pre-reflexive consciousness of man.

II. THE NEW HORIZON OF LIFE AND ITS EXPLICIT EXPRESSION

Logically, prior to revelation and faith, human existence is a mystery which cannot be fully explained, and therefore is fundamentally a religious quest. Since, like man himself, self-understanding develops within history, the future dimension plays a very pregnant role in man's search for himself. We have already said that the absolute relation to God is a depth-dimension in and of the human, historical relations—with one's fellowmen and the world. The Absolute contains a promise for the man living in history, and this promise appears on the plane of human existence as expectation or openness to the future, even with respect to the religious quest which man is, and to which of himself he can give no answer.

If now within human history—a relative reality—not only relative meanings appear, but, in the historical Jesus, the Christ, an absolute meaning also appears and can be grasped historically , then this by its very nature is a wholly new qualification of the transcendental depth-dimension of our human experience; then the transcendental horizon of life escapes, as it were, from its indistinct anonymity: the transcendental relation then, as it were, allows its face to be seen; it breaks open into a theologal life-horizon. This new horizon is based on the active and universal saving will of God who offers himself to all men as a gratuitous gift. The element of theologal experience, in which the God of salvation—albeit indistinctly—offers himself as grace, thus manifests itself as being based on "sanctifying grace," in the mode either of interiorizing acceptance or of alienating refusal. That which Thomas calls "interna vocatio ad credendum,"[3] the "instinctus interior invitans nos ad credendum" and which in an unthematic way transposes the transcendental horizon of our life into a theologal horizon, this is thematically expressed in and through man's religious life in various groping and faltering confessions of faith, and even more explicitly so, under God's special inspiration, in and through the Judeo-Christian salvation history, so that in the Scripture and in the Church of Christ we have a divine guarantee for the veracity of this thematic expression. The preaching of the church, the church's confession of faith, and the Christian dogma are the explicit content of theologal experience, all this under the guidance of God, who brought it to thematic expression through the prophets and especially through the man Jesus. Theologal, then, means that the implicit transcendental horizon of life is itself clarified in and through *categorial* realities, that is realities which exist in history.[4] The categorial in created life, with its own mundane meaning, is founded upon and constituted by the implicit transcendental relation to God. However, in the theologal life, that is, in the religion of revelation, categorial realities immediately manifest the implicit mystery of God, in the face of which the self-understanding of man had found itself powerless. The categorial thus becomes the visible form which interprets the mystery of God. In other words: in and through God's gratuitous, absolute self-communication, the Absolute as mystery is given to us directly as the horizon of our experience, yet still it can only be explicitated in categorial forms, and hence only indirectly. In our natural consciousness the wholly-Absolute is never given to us directly; it remains a "quo"-consciousness, not a "quod"-consciousness; that is to say: it remains an enlightening horizon of our consciousness-in-and-through-the world-of-men-and-objects, and therefore the uncomprehended and incomprehensible background of our dialogue with our fellowmen and the world. In God's self-revelation on the contrary, and thus in the life of faith, the Absolute, while remaining mystery, nevertheless approaches us immediately: it gives itself to us directly as a dimension of experienced reality, even though still it can only be explicitated indirectly. In other words, in the faith, the Absolute is no longer only "background," but foreground, even though it can be experienced only in faith and thus in veiled presence through an indirect thematic expression: a theologal way of existence or communion with God, thematically expressed, however, in and through categorial factors (concepts, images and worldly realities). Man can become present to himself—even to that very depth where he can come to the explicit natural affirmation of God—only in and through a profane world of inter-human relations on earth. Likewise, man can become present to himself, at that depth at which he is innerly addressed by God's offer of grace, only if he goes out into a world which is not only a humanized world or a human history, but also a history of salvation. Only in and through a history of salvation does man become present to himself in theologal communion with the living God.

However, the change from the transcendental to the theologal horizon of life intrinsically qualified this indirect expression: the Absolute is then given directly in its intrinsic mystery. For instance, Christ is the Son of God. By this fact religiousness is no longer restricted to the religious character of the experience of worldly reality itself, but finds also its own field of experience: in preaching, in liturgical gatherings, and so forth.

The fact of revelation means that God himself reveals, opens up to a man, the religious depth-dimension of man himself. It means that He reveals man to himself, defines as it were what being human should be. But He does this precisely by revealing the absolute ground of man's being, namely Himself, God. He reveals himself by laying open, revealing to man, the depth-dimension of man himself. Consequently, the revelation of salvation reaches man in the very core of his self-understanding. Revelation of salvation and divine clarification of human self-understanding are correlative: God sketches the "theo-logy" by revealing an "anthropology;" He reveals the anthropology by sketching the theology.

Thus in one and the same subject—man—occurs the historical self-understanding and the divine revelation of man to himself through God's absolute self-communication. This occurs in such a way that revelation presupposes, as condition of its own meaningfulness, man's search for himself. Therefore, faith, confession of faith, and dogma can function meaningfully only in human self-understanding. The explicitation and thematic expression of the elements of theologal experience immediately takes form in propositions, expressions and images which come from the current worldview and vision of man. Human self-understanding is thus an inner dimension of revelation itself. As it is heard by man, revelation naturally grows into theology —pre-reflexive, reflexive, or methodical and scientific theology. And this transition is an intrinsic element of man's faith itself.

Consequently, theological Dogmatics must keep pace with man's historically conditioned self-understanding, at any rate if the preaching of the Christian faith wants to give existentially relevant answers to the problems of human existence. But there is more. By virtue of God's universally active saving will, there is no longer a purely natural human life: wherever men are found, their life is determined by a theologal life-horizon which they have (albeit implicitly) accepted or refused. Consequently, the concrete experience of existence is really a *locus theologicus,* because that experience unavoidably involves a Christian outlook on life—even though perhaps unthematic. Therefore, philosophical self-understanding also—even when interpreted in an atheistic perspective—is, in fact, a *locus theologicus* for the believer, and not only an extrinsic *usus philosophiae in S. Doctrina.* Nevertheless, it does remain true that human existence which is Jesus, the Christ—an existence coming out of the Old Testament People of God moulded by biblical piety, and his self-

awareness which interprets human existence in and through his
unconditional abandonment to God and fellowmen—that human existence of Christ is the only authorized *locus theologicus*.
Therefore, the experience of human existence as a "locus theologicus" is legitimate and valid only insofar as it is measured
by the "norma non normanda," namely, by the human existence
of Christ, the Son of God, according to the apostolic witness of
Holy Scripture.

All this points out how deeply the historically conditioned
and thus evolving image of man and the world and human self-
understanding encroach upon the explicit Christian faith as
the thematic expression of the content of an element of theologal
experience which, in itself, remains irrevocably unthematic.
There is a good thomistic saying which states that the confession
of faith does not terminate in the dogmatic expression of the
content of faith, but in the saving reality itself. *"Actus credentis
non terminatur ad enuntiabile, sed ad rem."*[5] In response to the
two tendencies which he was considering—one of which maintained that faith refers directly to the formulation, to the intel-
ligible expression of faith, whereas the other said that the affirmation of faith reaches the saving reality itself[6]—Thomas said, at
least in his ultimate synthesis as found in the *Summa,* that there
is truth in both these tendencies.[7] Human judgment attains
reality itself, but in such a way that this intellectual contact with
reality remains implicit in the judgment: it is made explicit
conceptually, but in this way the concrete experience of reality
is expressed only to a certain extent and inadequately. That is
to say that our concepts of faith, and our explicit confession of
faith, can only grasp reality in the element of theologal experience which is really but inadequately expressed in the confession of faith. Thus the truth is contained not only in the pre-
reflexive implicit experience; if grasped in that element, truth is
also reached in the reflexively formulated data of faith. However, this formulation can never completely grasp nor exhaust

the pre-reflexive content of faith. The Judeo-Christian salvation history is precisely the history, accomplished under God's direction, of the explicitation of theologal experience which in itself is implicit and unthematic. At this level, God as absolute self-giving is experienced in faith. However, the distinction between "nature" and "supernature," between the transcendental and the theologal horizon of life, is never explicitly perceived in the experience; this distinction becomes reflexively explicit only through revelation and reflexive Christian self-understanding.

III. CONTINUOUS REINTERPRETATION OF DOGMA IN FAITHFUL OBEDIENCE TO THE SAVING ACTS AND WORD OF GOD

Because of the historical situation of human self-understanding, and the historical content of the Christian revelation, the Christian confession of faith and its thematic expression in theology also exist in history.

Thus, the very first question of theological reflection remains: what does God's revealed word tell us as it lives in the Church and is authentically interpreted by the Church's teaching authority? But we would be sadly mistaken if we were thus to conclude that the theologian would first have to "bracket" his contemporary thought in order to determine beforehand what precisely is revealed and only then, in a second stage, translate this into contemporary language. That is quite simply impossible. Contemporary thinking goes hand in hand with the examination, for example, of what the Tridentine dogma of the grace of justification or the dogma of transubstantiation means for us. Every "bracketing" of this modern problematic excludes *a priori* a precise interpretation, for example, of these Tridentine dogmas. The medieval translation of the mystery of faith was no problem for the man of the Middle Ages; it is a problem for me, since I live in another intellectual climate and my self-

understanding is different from that of someone in the Middle
Ages. I cannot correctly evaluate the dogmatic meaning of the
ancient Councils if I act as though history had stood still since
Chalcedon or Trent—as though I, a believing Catholic but also
a twentieth century man, were not different from the ancient or
the man of the Middle Ages, different also in my believing;
as though the catholic faith—remaining identical with itself
through history—were not involved in history. If that were the
case, my faith would only be a concern with documents and
monuments, and not with the eschatological saving work of
God who has revealed himself to us precisely in the history of
mankind in search of itself; He his revealed himself as *Theos
pros hemas,* as God-for-us in the man Jesus, the Christ: Son
of God.

The history of theology teaches us that the purely material
repetition of a formulation of the faith which was worked out
in another intellectual climate is always dangerous; in any
case, we can then hardly speak of a living and existentially
relevant affirmation of faith. On the other hand: we never find
the Word of God *à l'état pur.* Expressions such as "the working
or clothing of the dogma," however correct when one reflects
on earlier formulations, are misleading in the last analysis. They
give the impression that we can "dress" and "undress" a dogma
with the ease with which children play at dressing dolls. What
for us now is an outdated mentality, an outdated image of man
and the world, so that we can make a distinction in the faith
of the past between what was actually affirmed and what was
only the form of expression, the clothing of that faith, this was
in former centuries a life and death question, a question of "to
be or not to be" in the affirmation of faith itself. Although every
thinker must be constantly aware of the insufficiency and in-
adequacy of his thought, we cannot expect of a man, existing
in a determinate climate of thinking and self-interpretation, that
he should set aside his own thought (his very flesh and blood)

and anticipate history. To set aside his way of thought would be equivalent to refusing to consider the mystery of faith as meaningful. In the past no one could have thought of the faith or expressed it any way differently than they did; with their manner of expression the dogma stood or fell . . . for them. They themselves were not explicitly conscious of this "clothing" aspect, and they could not have been. They didn't have to for that matter.

Only when the intellectual climate starts to change and man comes to a different self-understanding in this world, only then is it meaningful to raise the question of the "clothing aspect" of the older formulation of dogmas, which in their core remain unchangeable. As human history moves ahead, the texts from the past reach a new fulfillment. For that reason, every generation can begin anew to study, for example, Plato or Augustine: the past keeps coming to life in a new way, and in such a way that the original Platonic or Augustinian sense and meaning of their works truly attain an inner fulfillment. It is, therefore, a matter of exegesis, not of inegesis. Hence, the re-reading and reinterpretation of the Bible is likewise never finished. Holy Scripture, re-read in every generation of the Church, for two thousand years now, in this way reveals her own meaning only gradually, thanks to the illumination which occurs when the past and the present come together, open to the future.

Because the faith functions in human self-understanding, and because both the believer's reflection and human self-understanding meet each other as it were in the same history, we cannot grasp the precise content of the faith, for example, of a Tridentine dogma, if, on the one hand we would want to "reconstruct" the Tridentine thought by excluding its old (in case: the Tridentine) essential categories in which the faith was then meaningfully considered, and if, on the other hand, we want to "lay aside" our new, present-day self-understanding. A twentieth century exposition of the content of faith as it was expressed, for example, in the Council of Trent, implies therefore that one identifies oneself and re-evaluates the particular content of faith, because we can never grasp it à l'état pur either. These hermeneutical principles seem to be especially important for ecumenism. A dogma is irrevocable and cannot be disposed of. But it can be assimilated into a new self-understanding, through which moreover it gets a new and different function in the whole of the totality of faith. And no one can see in advance what consequences this can have. To posit the possibility of taking into account in advance cultural developments in self-understanding would entail the negation of the genuine historicity within the dynamic self-identity of the dogma. The Vatican Council II has already shown us how the irrevocable catholic dogma, functioning in a new self-understanding and in new formal categories of thought, has brought Christians really closer to one another. Men are now rightly beginning to look for the non-theological factors which have increased the gulf between Christians and made the restoration of unity more difficult. Rightly so. But, in my opinion, it is even more urgently necessary to reinterpret the irrevocable catholic dogma, so that its original, unassailable meaning will begin to function existentially in the new contemporary self-understanding. A "rewriting" for example, of the whole Tridentine dogma in the light of contemporary human self-expression, would mean in my opinion an enormous step forward ecumenically. Personally I had hoped that this would be done by the Council, but the time was apparently not ripe for it.

Even apart from the ecumenical importance, it is urgent that within the Church we Catholics allow the faith to function in this new self-understanding. A clear doubt about representations of the faith which has not been resolved in the church's confession of faith as it functions in a proper image of man and the world, can in the long run begin to gnaw away at the church's confession of faith itself,—such as we now see happening everywhere around us in the difficulties of faith with which especially the young are struggling.

I have stated only general principles here. May they suffice to urge all theologians to work harder than ever, and thus speed up the process of finding existentially relevant answers, in faith, to the real problems.

NOTES

1 The word *"theologal"* is a neologism which refers to the communion with the living God. This communion surpasses the "natural" capacities of man, and is possible only through the gratuitous self-communication of God. Consequently, it is equivalent to the traditional word "supernatural" which, however, refers explicitly only to the surpassing of human powers. Thus, I prefer the term "theologal" to express this mutual communion or inter-subjectivity of God and man. "Theologal" is used here in distinction to "transcendental" which refers to the implicit depth-dimension of "nature" (as this is explained in the text, pp. 1–3), that is to say, the nature of man is in itself a transcendental relation to God.

2 "Unthematic" experience refers to a primary depth experience which is referred to in the text as "pre-reflexive" and/or "unthematic"—meaning that this experience and the reality which is experienced *cannot* be adequately expressed or "objectified" in what we will call "thematic" expression. This *"thematic"* expression, in turn, means the reflexive explicitation in concepts, images, and/or historical realities—of that primary depth experience.

3 *Sum. theol* II–II, q.2, a.9, ad 3; *Quodl.* II, q.4, a.6, ad/et 3.

4 The neologism *"categorial"* refers in general to the existing created realities of this world and of history. It is used here in distinction to "theologal" which was explained above (cfr. footnote 1).

5 II–II, q.1, a. 2, ad 2.

6 l. c. in c.

7 "Et ideo utrumque vere opinatum fuit apud antiquos" (II-II, q.7, a.2, c.)

JOSEPH SITTLER

The Principal Problem for Protestant Theology Today

The title of this brief essay, "The Principal Problem for Protestant Theology Today," contains several assumptions that ought to be investigated at the outset. The term "Protestant Theology," if regarded as designative of the theology Protestants actually produce, spans a spectrum that reaches all the way from continuing biblicistically oriented work of a very sober and respectable nature, on the one hand, to biblically centered but radically critical theological formulations on the other—the latter principally proceeding from reflections engendered by the force of the hermeneutical knot at the heart of biblical interpretation. Whoever would speak reportorially about Protestant theology must make a judgment; and this judgment would inevitably be assailed from within the Protestant family.

The second assumption, that one can confidently specify what, within the spectrum alluded to, addresses the mind of the Protestant theologian with such an urgency as to demand that its investigation constitute his principal task, is also a perilous assumption. Whoever proposes a judgment about the matter will be forced to defend his judgment. This perilous way of life among Protestant theologians, while depriving them of the serenity their hearts desire, has nevertheless, and in a curious way, been one of the liveliest components in Protestant theological work since Schleiermacher. *The Christian Faith,* for instance, delivers its message in the course of defending the proposal that the chosen judgment about method is, indeed, the correct one. One has only to study Karl Barth's magnificent essays on *Protestant Theology in the Nineteenth Century* to become aware of how profoundly the problem of theological methodology has dominated the last century and a half of Protestant theological effort.

But having reminded ourselves of the difficulty of the wide term *Protestant theology,* and having seen that the methodological search so long engaged in by Protestant thinkers is a kind of admission that the naming of the concrete task for theology today is equally difficult, one is not thereby relieved of the necessity to make a judgment; he is only chastened and sobered in his efforts to do that.

. I propose, in a moment, to say clearly what I think that task to be. But several considerations must precede such a statement. The first consideration is this: despite the range and variety of Protestant thought in the four hundred and fifty years since the Reformation there does persist in it a center which cannot be displaced, because this center was not arbitrarily chosen; it was constituted a center precisely in virtue of that effort to reform the Church around what was affirmed to be the core and substance of the Gospel. When, therefore, a Protestant theologian reflects upon the task of theology in any age he has the obligation to stand critically within that center, to enquire and ever re-enquire into scripture, history, and the actual life of faith, to be sure whether that starting-point be in fact the right one, and out of a conviction and obedience ever freshly renewed, elaborate for the passing generations and with all possible depth, urgency and relevance an understanding of the Christian faith.

And more, when a Protestant theologian stands in the mainstream of the Reformation he recalls—if indeed he has to recall!

—that the Reformation Church-communities came into existence through the agency of men who were sons of the Church. These men were reformers, not repudiators; their intention as sons of the Church was, in the name of the Church and for the sake of the Church, to celebrate the truth of the gospel for the right obedience and fuller truth of the Church-catholic.

This recollection is not only a recollection! It is a theological fact that today further complicates the effort to specify in strictly Protestant terms and from a strictly Protestant point of view the present task. For just as the idea of a self-conscious theological tradition over against Roman Catholicism must be modified by such recollection and practice, events of the last hundred years have further qualified the legitimacy of a radically Protestant theological task. In that statement I am simply attending to events that have penetrated both traditions at such a depth and with such transforming force as to confront both with theological tasks so novel and urgent as to give them common work to do which may perhaps be more clear and commanding than their separate pasts are solidified into divergence, or their separate past issues-of-debate any longer germane.

Such events as have penetrated both traditions can be clearly seen and precisely stated: a marked slackening in the older alliances of theological method with this or that philosophical tradition; the powerful reentrance into the formation of fundamental ideas and theological terms of the vibrant, enormously illuminating and rich biblical world of thought, world of language, world of experienced relations between God and man, the fellow-man, the world-as-history, the world-as-nature; the gradual but inexorable effect upon theological method created by the changed situation in which the church and the world face one another; the current apologetical situation which forces the theologian (and the preacher-witness) to make the proposal of the truth of the Christian faith to the world in close and rigorously critical relation to all phenomenologically ordered disciplines.

The degree to which the understanding of the Protestant
theological task I have attempted to describe is characteristic of
the common life of the non-Roman "ecclesial" communities is
a separate topic. But I think it is on the whole correct as regards
the most responsible theologians.

A judgment, then, thus qualified, about the peculiar task of
Protestant theology today. But how reluctantly one makes such
a judgment! Reflect for a moment upon the word—judgment!
Such reflection dare not be excessive lest it

> ... be sicklied o'er by the pale cast of thought
> And lose the name of action!

A judgment is an announcement at the end of reflection. If one
remembers the madly various, accidental, non-consecutive elements that constitute reflection he gains a salutary lesson in
theological humility! For in every judgment made about religio-
historical facts and forces one brings some things forward and
leaves others recessive. He does this, not as he is tempted to
suppose, in virtue of some celestial elevation above the accidents
of time, place, circumstance, personal experience, nature and
disposition, cultural affinities—but as a traceable function of
these. "Non intratur in veritatem nisi per caritatem" (There is
no entrance into truth save by love). In a plain everyday factic
sense that is true, although in a context other than St. Augustine
intended in his epigram. For there is a mystery to the mind's
attention. We do love, attend to, are affected by, have our emo-
tional resources stirred into life by quite particular ills, needs,
distortions, threats to the health of human life. And the practice
of theological discussion would be a more blithe, humane interchange, if in more becoming humility we steadily acknowledged
this. The principal task for Protestant theology today is to
learn how to make the proposal of grace to a mentality that is
shaped predominantly by ever deepening and enlarging transactions with the world-as-nature. Just as "men's minds tend to

follow the fortunes of their bodies with an absolute seriousness,"
so dimensions of possibility, the range of reflections, the agenda
of viable relations, and the sufficiency of older ways of knowing
—all of these undergo both enlargement and shrinkage in a
time whose interesting and most creative intellectual programs
are related to man-nature transactions.

A recent essay speaks of our "culture as 'ageric' (from the
Latin *agere*, to act), denoting a culture that makes a distinction
between dormancy and activity, and insists on doing things as
a way of conceiving time. This mode of seeing reality is most
characteristic of North America and northern Europe. In certain
other cultures no distinction is made between being passive
and being active. Hence, time passes in any case, and it makes
no difference whether one does something or not. But Ameri-
cans and other ageric moderns are different. With us we have
to work to get ahead. We do not get ahead automatically
(Sellers, James: "The Almost Chosen People," *Journal   of
Religion,* The University of Chicago, Vol. XLV, No. 4, 1965).

The depth to which reflection about the nature, structure,
needs, possibilities of the self is penetrated by this generally un-
criticized assumption is becoming evident, for instance, in the
growing debate about the proposal of a guaranteed annual
wage for all adult citizens in the United States. That debate
has not centered upon economic, social or legal aspects of the
proposal but upon what is affirmed to be the threat to moral
life inherent in it. The assumption, considered so clear and
strong as not to be arguable, is that man's deepest meaning, a
reflection of the *Imago Dei*, is both found and realized in his
operational relations with the potentialities of the world-as-
nature. Contemporary men in a technological society have so
absolutely fused what the theologians call anthropology with
operational identity that questions of being are not even statable
in terms other than those that specify being as doing.

Of the genesis and development of this cultural modality it

is not possible to speak at this moment; it is both possible and necessary to inquire what criticism of traditional Christian teaching is implied in it, what tasks it places upon theological reformulation, and even—to think ahead to its fullest implication —what reinterpretation of eschatology might be demanded.

It does not seem to be the case that any tradition in Christian theology has taken the massive measure of the modification in anthropology disclosed by ageric man; and the theological studies which do essay this task remain conceptually locked in a vocabulary of an older time, and often move about in a piety unshattered by the social actuality of men in such corporate endeavors as deeply qualify conventional notions of privacy, individuality, work, community.

The conciliar document, *The Church in the World Today,* is properly designated a *Pastoral* Constitution. It is precisely that: its aim is to articulate the awareness of the Church about the realities of the common life to which the Church pastorally wishes and must learn to relate herself. The Constitution is wise and compassionate, sometimes penetratingly diagnostic in its survey. But it remains, as perhaps its self-imposed limitations required, almost completely descriptive. This designation is not intended as a criticism of the statement; clear sight is the precondition of appropriate theological formulation.

But theological formulation and reformulation there must be; and if descriptive responsibility is understood as prologomenon, and operates as lure into deeper theological analysis, the larger task of renewal is well served.

If, then, one attempts to state the capital theological task which ensues—informed by, spurred by such a Constitution— what rubric is large enough to order and contain the fresh thinking that is required? It is no accident that the doctrine of Creation in theological efforts by both Roman Catholic and non-Roman Catholic scholars has moved to the very center of attention. Such a movement clearly signifies that man's transactions with the world-as-nature are not adequately addressed by the Christian faith when the gift-character, meaning, duty toward and the fate of the creation is elaborated under the article of Redemption. Shifts among topics whereby they are differently ordered in the course of theological history are eloquent with meaning. The Council's decision, for instance, to place its teaching about Mary within the Constitution on The Church is somewhat more than a convenience in Table of Contents or a device whereby to reduce the number of schemata.

The present concern with the doctrine of the Creation can be easily accounted for. With a singular and startling velocity the penetration into the nature and process of the physical world raced, from the late Medieval groping efforts at an empirical scientific method, to this moment when the macrocosm is deepeningly unfolded to man's gaze. The cosmos, from the infinitely far and vast to the incredibly minute, lies ever more intricately exposed, so full of mystery that sober doubts are entertained as to an intellectual correspondence between mind and time-space reality. But patterns of coherence are nevertheless visible; and science, begetting a huge technology, has now proceeded to the point where practical operations with nature, built upon proximate models of a possible reality, have transformed the conditions of human life on the earth.

What this transformation, increasing exponentially, does to the personal self in solitude and in the matrix of social relations, and in the new forms of self-actualization imposed by corporate management of economic and civil existence, is nothing short of a requirement for an anthropology attentive to it. This same transformation imposes upon Christian theology the task to re-examine every basic term in its vocabulary, unfolding these terms in contrapuntal interchange between Word of God, the riches of Christian thought from the beginning, and the needs, thoughts, operational space of men for whom a geocentric frame for thought is no longer possible, and whose notions of history are complicated by what Carl von Weiszächer, Teilhard de Chardin and others have explicated as a nature-history symbiosis of an incredible richness. As men's minds follow the gaze of their eyes into interstellar and sub-atomic space it is not to be expected that questions of purpose, process, meaning and self-hood can be addressed by theological energies proposed in categories appropriate to an earlier time in a simpler universe.

Against such a background it would be ludicrous to suppose that any suggested program for theological work called forth by changes of such magnitude should be called "Protestant"! Indeed, it may come about that the unity of Christ's Church will be given, not so directly to our efforts to find a common past in a common core, but rather will be given as a gift to our intellectual and moral and mission-obedience as together we make our way as a grace-attended pilgrimage into the shadowy future.

There is, however, in one sense, a particularly Protestant task; it weighs upon that theological community with a particular urgency. The doctrine of grace as that doctrine was elaborated by the Reformers of the sixteenth century was characterized by a Christological focus, a vitality and a freedom that incessantly presses at the borders of every other doctrine: Revelation, Ecclesiology, Sacraments. It is precisely Protestant concentration upon the Godly freedom of grace which has made it creatively difficult for Protestant Christianity to achieve that clear definition in doctrinal statement which Roman Catholic theology has noted—and frequently lamented. It is an interesting field for reflection to ask what relation obtains between the extended Roman Catholic sacramental theology, the developments in Mariology—and Roman Catholic efforts to contain within systematic teaching the power, presence, ever-recreative energies of grace.

The substance and scope of what I regard as our common, and perhaps in a limited sense, peculiarly Protestant task can be summarized in a series of questions.

1. What relation is there between the world-and-nature-engagement of contemporary man and the classically elaborated doctrine of grace as this doctrine was given its western form by Augustine?

2. What are the biblical dimensions of the meaning and power of the grace of God which "came in Jesus Christ" and have these dimensions been unfolded with a fullness sufficient for a time whose questions and needs transcend the understanding of grace as forgiveness, as restoration, as divine action for moral guilt.

3. If the doctrine of creation in the career of Israel's dealings with her God followed the doctrine of the divine redemption—became, as it were, a religious celebration in absolute terms of the power and goodness of God—is it not possible that the reality of grace that Christianly we know as centered in Jesus Christ must now be elaborated to a cosmic scope, and confessed to inhere as the power, presence, goodness of God in the Creation—particularly the Creation as technologically transformed.

4. If, to older designations of man as *homo-sapiens, homo politicus, homo ludens,* etc., we must now add the term *homo operator* in order to acknowledge the extent to which selfhood and identity are specified by novel engagements with and transformations of nature—is it not urgent that the farthest reaches of Christology "his purpose which he set forth in Christ as a plan for the fullness of time, to unite all things in him, things in heaven and things on earth" (Eph. 1:10) must now be freshly and more broadly declared to world-administering man, in order that secular knowledge and operations may be "Christologically" interpreted and ethicized, and to the end that proliferating power may be secured against catastrophe and its power and promise confessed to be a huge theatre "to that praise of his glorious grace" (Eph. 1:16)?

J.B. METZ

The Church and the World

If the precise point of view from which this subject will be treated here is to be clear, some preliminary remarks are needed.

First: for the theologian councils are never an end, with which he can be content, but rather a beginning. They bring forth new tasks and consequently do not diminish, but increase theological responsibility. Therefore, although we may admire the progress made by the Second Vatican Council, we should not overlook its limitations and its contingent character. For example, did not the Church in this council speak too exclusively of herself, in a narcissistic way, looking into a mirror, rather than through an open window into the world, to find her true countenance? Moreover, since the Church has evidently not spoken of everything of which she could have and should have spoken, it would be false and dangerous if theologians would limit themselves during the next fifty years to a mere commentary on the various constitutions of this council. For this reason, my remarks on "The Church and the World" will concentrate not so much on what the council said as on what the council did *not* say.

The second preliminary remark relates directly to our topic and its scope. Since the extensive scope of this topic can easily lead to superficiality, I will limit my treatment in two ways. The

69

first limitation results from the fact that I write as a professor of fundamental theology. This discipline serves the responsibility of hope according to 1 Pet. 3, 15: "Always be prepared to make a defense to anyone who calls you to account for the hope that is in you. . . . " Thus fundamental theology seeks to explicate the faith in a manner corresponding to the present historical modes of human understanding. It does this, not in order to submit itself to the ruling modes of thought, but in order to enter into a fruitful conflict with these modes of thought. I will therefore treat this topic of "The Church and the World" as a problem which belongs to the responsibility of the Christian faith as confronted with the present historical situation and its modes of thought. The usual conflict between the thought of the times and the thought of the Christian faith often forces the individual Christian to walk through the crucial tests of his faith alone and without the adequate help of theology for his present situation.

The second limitation of my treatment results from the horizon[1] in which I would like to explain and to develop concretely the relation of the Christian faith to the world. This horizon is the future. And it reveals the world as history, history as final history (*Endgeschichte*), faith as hope, and theology as eschatology. This horizon characterizes the attempt of theology to surpass and to go beyond the modern transcendental, personalistic, and existential theology without disregarding its valuable insights. This transcendental, personalistic and existential theology has correctly emphasized the role of the human person in contrast to the mere objectivistic viewpoint of scholastic theology. It has brought the Christian faith into a proper relationship to human existence and subjectivity. However, this theology faces two dangers. On the one hand, this anthropological theology tends to limit the faith by concentrating on the *actual* moment of the believer's personal decision. The *future* is then all but lost. It becomes only another name for the intractable factors of the present decision. On the other hand, this anthropological theology tends to become private and individualistic. It fails to bring into sufficient prominence the social and political dimensions of the believer's faith and responsibility.

After these preliminary remarks, we turn to our topic "The Church and the World." I would like to develop three theses: 1) First, a thesis on the modern understanding of the world, with its stress on the future and its operational orientation. 2) Secondly, a thesis on the scriptural source of our understanding of the world,—an understanding rooted in the promises of God. 3) Thirdly, a thesis on the resulting notion of faith as a creative and militant relationship to the world understood in the light of God's promises.

I

First Thesis. The modern man's understanding of the world is fundamentally oriented toward the future. His mentality therefore is not primarily contemplative but operative.

First of all, the modern era persistently strives after the New (*das Novum*). This era began with the "new" world and this new world stamped the slogan of its program on the dollar bill: "*novus* ordo seclorum." This striving after the new is the predominate spirit of the social, political and technical revolutions of our time. The men of this era are attracted and fascinated *only* by the future, i.e., by that which has never been. "This fascination with the future transforms the existing and subsisting reality into a changing and a challenging reality, so that the real of this reality emerges as its possibilities for the future."[2]

Since the modern man's "passion is for the possible" (Kierkegaard), the direct force of tradition has declined. The old quickly turns into the obsolete. "The good old days" have lost their appeal. The golden age lies not behind us, but before us: it is not re-created in the memories of our dreams, but created in the desires of our imagination and heart. Man's relationship to the past becomes increasingly a mere esthetic, romantic and archaic interest, and by his archival curiosity for the past he acknowledges the past as something antiquated. In other words, the present mentality has a merely historical (*historisch*) relationship to the past, but it has an existential (*geschichtlich*) relationship to the future.

Secondly: in his striving toward the future the modern man no longer experiences the world as an imposed fate, or as a sovereign sacrosanct nature confining him, but rather as a quarry —as the raw material—with which he builds his own "new world." He not only alters the world and forms it into the stage props for his own historical drama, but he also dominates the world through technology, and thereby secularizes it.[3]

Thirdly: How should theology relate itself to this new world-situation? Some theologians play the ostrich and wish for the situation to pass. Others have taken the situation seriously and used various forms of dialectical theology to relate christianity and the world (especially students and friends of Karl Barth: e.g. F. Gogarten and D. Bonhoeffer). Since the new understanding of the world has questioned and even thrown away many of the tried and faithful thought-forms of the Christian faith, these perceptive theologians emphasize the radical otherness of the faith—its radical difference from this world. And in this paradoxical understanding of the Christian faith by the modern theologies of secularization, dialectical theology celebrates a victory in the theology of secularization. For example, the use of the dialectical theology of Barth, Gogarten and Bonhoeffer gives evidence to its ambiguous character in Harvey Cox's important book, *The Secular City*. He attempts in the first part to emphasize the total transcendence and otherness of God and the Christian faith, and in the second part of his book to unite eschatology and social revolution. But, I ask, how can the gospel of the totally-other God flow into a social-gospel: in other words,

how does Cox unite the first and second part of his book?[4] In
order to demonstrate the insufficiency of this reaction of "dialectical theology" we will examine in a more precise manner what
has actually occurred in the modern age's new understanding
of the world. The "World-Beyond" (*Jenseits*) and the "Heaven
above us" has not only become hidden, but seems to have disap-
peared. (What is hidden can indeed be powerful and near!)
Slowly but constantly the world has lost its glimmer of divinity:
we have this world in our hands and projects. No longer is the
world recognized as the numinous vestibule of heaven. No longer
do we directly discover in and on the world the footsteps of God,
the *vestigia Dei*, but rather we see only the footsteps of men, the
vestigia hominis, and *his* actions of changing the world. We
apparently encounter in and on the world only ourselves and
our own possibilities. The shining glow of the "world above"
and the "world beyond" has dimmed. It seems as if it can no
longer enlighten the spirit of man and enkindle his enthusiasm.
What moves the man of today is not the commitment for the
"world above" but the commitment to build a *new* world (or, if
you will, to build a "great society"). This engagement and commitment to the future does challenge and appeal to the man of
today, who otherwise seems so disenchanted and so a-religious.

Fourthly: both in the West and the East every impressive
Weltanschauung and humanistic ideology of today is oriented
toward the future. We need only to think about Marxism and
its theory of the classless society, according to which man himself
produces his own future and society: The desired perfection of
a successful mankind does not lie "above us" but "before us."
The total modern critique against religion, beginning with the
marxistic critique, can be reduced to this common denominator:
Christianity, as well as religion in general, is powerless in the
face of this primacy which the future occupies in the modern
mentality. Our present age is therefore conceived of by these
critics as the time of the liquidation of the religious mentality,

as the beginning of a post-religious era, in which every belief in
a transcendent God is exposed as a mere speculative conception
of the mind, to be cast off and replaced by an active and
operative orientation toward the future.

Fifthly: What does the Christian faith say or do in the face
of this situation? How does the Christian account for *his* hope?
Can he understand the world in a way that does not flatly exclude his faith, that does not force his theology into an irrelevant
and incomprehensible paradox? Can the Christian faith perhaps
find itself *anew* in this situation and *grow* in the midst of making
the world? I believe it can, but under one condition: only if the
Christian theologian becomes alarmed about a loss of eschatology, and only if he becomes disturbed about the neglect and
unawareness of the future in his theology. This neglect is so
persistent that, for example, the so-called *existential* interpretation of the New Testament involves only the re-actualization
and the re-presentation of the past in the present moment of
religious decision. The present alone dominates. There is no
real future! *Exempli gratia:* Bultmann! We must bring together
that which has been so long disastrously separated: namely
Transcendence (God) and Future, because this orientation
toward the future is demanded by the biblical faith and message
itself. Only then can the faith enter into a fruitful conflict and
discussion with our modern era's passion for the future. Only a
theology which has re-possessed its orientation to the future can
seriously ask: where does this primacy of the future come from,
which primacy impregnates the modern mentality and the political, social, and technical revolutions of our times? What is the
origin of this primacy of the future? What is its foundation?[5]

II

Second Thesis. The orientation of the modern era to the
future, and the understanding of the world as history, which

results from this orientation, is based upon the biblical belief in the promises of God. This biblical faith demands that theology be eschatology.

I can naturally give only a few explanatory comments to this thesis. My direct appeal to the statements of the Sacred Scriptures is not arbitrary, but is based upon the results of recent biblical research in Germany, which in its post-Bultmannian period is bringing back into focus the Old Testament, and, secondly, is using the Old Testament as means of understanding the New Testament.

First of all, recent exegetical researches indicate that the words of Revelation in the Old Testament are not primarily words of statement or of information, nor are they mainly words of appeal or of personal self-communication by God, but they are *words of promise*. Their statement is announcement, their announcement is proclamation of what is to come, and therefore the abrogation of what is. (Perhaps the German would more clearly express my thought: *Die Aussage ist Ansage, die Verkündigung ist Ankündigung des Kommenden und dadurch Aufkündigung des Bestehenden*). This dominant proclamation and word of promise initiates the future: it establishes the covenant as the solidarity of the Israelites who hope, and who thereby experience the world for the first time as a history which is oriented to the future. This Hebrew experience and thought stands in contrast to Greek thought, which understands the world not as a history oriented to the future, but as a closed cosmos or as a subsisting world of nature. This Hebrew thought is contained in those important passages of the Old Testament which are impregnated with a pathos for the new (*das Novum*), for the new time and for the new coming world, i.e., for the new as that which *never* was. Greek thought, in contrast to Hebrew thought,[6] considers that which has never been as intrinsically impossible, since for the Greeks there is "nothing new under the sun." Everything which will come in the future is only a variation of the past and an

actualization or confirmation of the *anamnesis*. History is therefore only the indifferent return of the same within the closed
realm of the eternal cosmos. Since the essence of history is here
considered as cyclic, history is seen as devouring her own children over and over again, so that there is nothing new in history,
and the essence of history reveals itself as nihilistic. We emphasize this contrast between the Hebrew and Greek understanding
of the world in order to show that the biblical viewpoint considers the world as a *historical* world, in so far as it is a world
"arising toward" God's promises under the responsibility of the
Israelites, who hope in these promises. This understanding is
reflected in the Genesis creation narratives, which were originally
narratives of God's promises (so that they therefore express not
merely a faith in a past creation, but a faith in the new creation
of God's promises). The revelation of God's name in *Exodus*
3, 14 also indicates that this eschatological horizon is the central
aspect of God's revelation. The expression "I am who I am" is
much better translated as "I will be who I will be." (So Gerhard
von Rad and Martin Buber and a footnote in the *RSV*.) According to this version God revealed himself to Moses more as
the power of the future than as a being dwelling beyond all
history and experience. God is not "above us" but "before us."
His transcendence reveals itself as our "absolute future." This
future is grounded in itself, and is self-possessed. It is a future
that is not erected out of the potentialities of our human freedom and human action. Rather, this future calls forth our potentialities to unfold themselves in history. Only such a future—
one that is more than just the projections of our abilities—can
call us to realize truly *new* possibilities, to become that which
has *never* existed. "I will be who I will be." The future proclaimed here does not get its power from our present wishes and
effort.[7] No, its power stems from itself: it belongs to itself. Only
thus can and does this future exert its stirring and liberating
power over *every* human present, over *every* generation.

Secondly: the New Testament message does not remove the faith's orientation toward the future or hope in the future as the necessary and essential structure of faith. "The firm belief in the nearness of the Kingdom, which Jesus proclaimed and initiated, effected such a concentration and mobilization toward the promised future, that everything of the mere past and of the mere present lost its relevance."[8] It would be moreover false to think that in the Christ-Event the future is entirely behind us, as if the future of the history after Christ only plays itself out, but does not *realize* itself. On the contrary, the Christ-Event intensifies this orientation toward the not yet realized future. The proclamation of the resurrection of Jesus, which can never be separated from the message of the crucifixion, is essentially a proclamation of promise which initiates the Christian mission. This mission achieves its future in so far as the Chrisitan alters and "innovates" the world toward that future of God which is definitely promised to us in the resurrection of Jesus Christ. The New Testament is therefore centered on hope—a creative expectancy—as the very essence of Christian existence.

Thirdly: in view of the above, the Christian has the responsibility to develop his faith's relationship to the world as a relationship of hope, and to explicate his theology as eschatology. Although theology has a tract on eschatology, it generally puts this eschatology in a corner well away from the center of theology in the treatise "on the last things." Eschatology lacks a vital relationship to the whole of theology and it thereby fails to be related to the theology of the world. Christian eschatology must come out of its corner, into which it was shoved by a theology which has forgotten the relevance of hope and of the future. Since Christians are simply defined by Paul as "those who have hope," should they not understand their theology in *every* aspect as eschatology, and as the responsibility of hope? Eschatology is not a discipline beside other disciplines, but that basic discipline which determines, forms, and shapes every theological statement, especially those concerning the world. The attempt to interpret theology in a totally existential or personalistic way is an important accomplishment of theology. I attempted in my *Christliche Anthropozentrik* to base this interpretation upon Thomas Aquinas. This existential-anthropological theology, however, easily becomes isolated from the world and history, when eschatology is not seen to be more basic to theology. Only in the eschatological horizon of hope does the world appear as history. Only in the understanding of world as history does the free action of man obtain its central position. Only this central position of human freedom initiates a legitimate christian anthropocentrism. The universal existential-anthropological viewpoint in the christian theology depends on the eschatological viewpoint. This is true, because only in the eschatological horizon of hope does the world appear as an *arising* reality, whose development or process is committed to the free action of man. In addition, Christology and Ecclesiology must also be explicated in this horizon of eschatology, so that they are not abbreviated to either mere existential-anthropological or objectivized and cosmological viewpoints. At this point we can only mention these considerations and aspects. We will however say a word concerning ecclesiology further below.

Fourthly: it would be tempting, and important, to indicate how the process of the so-called secularization of the world was only possible because the world itself was experienced and understood in the eschatological horizon of hope. The world appears in this horizon not as a fixed and sacrosanct reality in a pre-established harmony, but as an *arising* reality, which can be innovated toward its future through the historically free actions of men. This universal alteration and innovation of the world through the offensive of human freedom characterizes that process, which we call secularization. We must however pass over this question here and proceed to our next thesis.

III

Third Thesis. The relationship between the Christian faith and the world should be characterized from a theological viewpoint as a creative and militant eschatology.

First: in explaining and establishing this thesis we would like to refer to a noteworthy sentence of St. Thomas Aquinas. He states in scholastic terminology that man does not have a natural last end (*finis ultimus naturalis*) *and* a supernatural last end (*finis ultimus supernaturalis*); but he has *only one* last end, namely, the future promised by God. From the viewpoint of the future the often used—perhaps too often used—distinction between the natural and the supernatural recedes into the background. In our relationship to the future we cannot be satisfied with a distinction which separates the natural future of the world from the supernatural future of the faith and of the Church. Both dimensions converge in our relationship to the future. In other words, since the hope of the Christian faith is orientated toward the future, it cannot fulfill itself in bypassing the world and the future of the world. And because this hope is responsible for the *one* promised future, it is therefore also responsible for the future of the world. The Christian faith hopes not only in itself, the Church hopes not only in itself, but they hope in the world.

Secondly: Is the biblical hope, however, really so radically orientated toward this one and undivided future? Is the Old Testament's conception of hope as a hope in the world and in its future still valid? Does not the New Testament require that this hope be impregnated with and accompanied by a renunciation of the world? It would indeed be unwise and an empty compromise with the spirit of the times, if we would suppress or minimize this motif of the New Testament's conception of

hope. I am aware of this motif and I consider it important—
even for our times. However, everything hinges upon a correct
understanding of what is properly meant by the renunciation of
the world. Because man can never live apart from the world or
worldless (i.e., without a world), this renunciation could never
be a mere flight out of the world. For such a flight would then
be a deceptive and illusory flight into an artificially isolated
world, which *de facto* is often the more comfortable religious
situation of yesterday. Not a flight *out* of the world, but a flight
with the world "forward" is the fundamental dynamism of the
Christian hope in its renunciation of the world. This renunciation is therefore a flight only out of that self-made world which
masters its present and lives solely out of its present, and whose
"time is always here" (cf. Jn. 7, 6). Christians should attentively
listen to Saint Paul when he exhorts them to renounce the world,
and when he urges them "not to be conformed to this world"
(cf. Rom. 12, 2). Paul does not criticize here the Christian's
solidarity with the world, but his conformity to the existing
world as enraptured with its own appearance, and as concerned
only with its self-glorification. Paul criticizes this world insofar
as it tries to determine its own future and to degrade this future
to a function of the powerful and power-hungry present. The
Apostle does not demand a one-sided (*undialektisch*) denial of
the world or a total refusal of engagement with the world. But
rather he urges the Christians to be prepared for a painful
estrangement from the present world situation. He exhorts them
to renounce the forgone conclusions of their times (cf. also Mt.
12, 29 ff.) and to abstain from the proud boastfulness and vanity
of the world (cf. I Cor. 1, 29). All of this, however, is done for
the sake of that future promised by God. The Christian is moved
to flee and to renounce the world not because he despises the
world but because he hopes in the future of the world as proclaimed in God's promises. And this hope gives him a responsibility for the world and its future—a future from which we can

too often isolate ourselves in forms of presumption and despair. This Christian renunciation of the world has its origin in the spirit of biblical hope and it serves the hope of all. It is the imitation of Christ at the hour of his crucifixion. This hour represents the singular affirmation of the world *and* the overcoming of the world. The Christian renunciation of the world takes on the servant's form of a crucified hope for the world. A faith which is guided by such a hope is primarily not a doctrine, but an initiative for the passionate innovating and changing of the world toward the Kingdom of God.

Thirdly: in this perspective we can more adequately define the relationship between Church and world. Despite the many discussions about the Church and the world there is nothing more unclear than the nature of their relationship to one another. The usual contemporary statements about the turning of the Church toward the world and about the positive evaluation of the world by the Church, etc., often add to the confusion and unclarity. Is the Church actually something other than the world? Is not the Church also world? Are not Christians—i.e., the Church—also of the world? Where is the Church turning to in her movement toward the world? The Church is of the world: In a certain sense the Church is the world: The Church is not Non-World (*Die Kirche ist nicht Nicht-Welt*). For it is *that world* which attempts to live from the promised future of God, and to call *that world* in question which understands itself only in terms of itself and its possibilities. The decisive relationship between the Church and the world is not spatial but temporal. The Church is the eschatological community and the exodus community. Its institutional and sacramental life is based on this eschatological character. The Eucharist is the sacrament of the Exodus; it is the commemoration of the death of Christ *as promise—donec dominus veniat*. The Church is not the goal of her own strivings; this goal is the Kingdom of God. "The Church always lives in a certain sense from the proclamation of her provisional character and from her historically progressive surrender to the coming Kingdom of God."[9] The Church has a hope and witnesses to a hope, but its hope is not in itself. It is rather a hope in the Kingdom of God as the future of the world. *Ecclesia est universale sacramentum spei pro totius mundi salute.*

Fourthly: How does the Church realize its mission to work for the future of the world? It cannot be by pure contemplation, since contemplation by definition relates to what has already become existent and to what actually exists. The future which the Church hopes for is not yet here, but is *emerging* and *arising* (*entstehend*). Therefore the hope which the Church sets in itself and in the world should be creative and militant. In other words, Christian hope should realize itself in a *creative and militant eschatology.* Our eschatological expectation does not look for the heavenly-earthly Jerusalem as that ready-made and existing, promised city of God. This heavenly city does not lie ahead of us as a distant and hidden goal, which only needs to be revealed. The eschatological City of God is *now* coming into existence, for our hopeful approach *builds* this city. We are workers building this future, and not just interpreters of this future. The power of God's promises for the future moves us to form this world into the eschatological city of God. The council in the Constitution on the Church says, *"Renovatio mundi . . . in hoc saeculo reali quodam modo anticipatur."* The Christian is a "co-worker" in bringing the promised universal era of peace and justice. The orthodoxy of a Christian's faith must constantly *make itself* true in the "orthopraxy" of his actions orientated toward the final future, because the promised *truth* is a truth which must be *made* (cf. Jn. 3, 21 ff.).

The Christian eschatology therefore is not—despite its popularity among the existential theologians—a mere presential or actual eschatology, in which the passion for the future exhausts itself in a mere "making present" of eternity in the actual moment of personal decision. Nor is Christian eschatology a mere passive waiting, in which the world and its time-span appear as a waiting room, where the Christian lounges around in lackadaisical boredom until God opens the door of his office and allows the Christian to enter. Christian eschatology is, however, a productive and militant eschatology, which gradually realizes itself. Since Christian hope (is that very hope which) does not only eat its stew but must also brew its stew. An eschatological faith and an engagement in the world do not exclude one another. Because Paul's words "do not conform to the world" do not only mean that we should change ourselves, "but also that we should in conflict and creative expectation change the pattern of this world in which we believe, hope and love. The hope of the Gospel has a polemical and a liberating relation to man's present and practical life and to the (social) conditions in which man leads his life."[10]

Fifthly: a theology of the world which is guided by this creative-militant eschatology cannot unfold itself in the style and categories of the old theological cosmology. Moreover, it cannot discharge its task with the categories of a mere transcendental, personal and existential theology because they are too individualistic and isolated. Since the theology of the world is not a mere theology of the cosmos nor a mere transcendental theology of the human person and existence, but a theology of the emerging political and social order, this theology of the world must be a *political theology*. An eschatologically orientated theology must place itself in communication with the prevailing political, social and technical utopias and with the contemporary maturing promises of a universal peace and justice. "The Christian salvation for which we hope is not only a personal salvation of one's soul or a mere rescuing of the individual from the evil world. Nor is it just a consolation for the personal conscience in temptation. It is *also* the achieving of an eschatological order of justice, the humanizing of man and the establishing of a universal peace. This "aspect" of our reconciliation with God has not been given sufficient prominence in the history of Christianity because Christians have no longer seen themselves in their true eschatological horizon, but have left the terrestial-eschatological expectations to the fanatics and enthusiasts."[11] In obeying its eschatological vocation Christianity should not establish itself as a ghetto-society or become the ideological protective shell for the existing society. Rather it should become the liberating and critical force of this one society. Christianity should not establish itself as a "micro-society" beside the "great secular society." Any separation of Church and State leading to a ghetto or to a micro-society is fatal. The *terminus a quo* of the Christian mission should be the secular society. On this society must the "osmotic pressure" of the Christian hope be exerted. The various institutions of Christianity find their legitimation and also their criterion in their eschatological mission. Wherever these institutions serve Christianity's self-protection more than its venture forward (*nach vorn*), then the bastions of these institutions should be dismantled.

And finally: the Christian's militant hope is not simply a "militant optimism." Nor does it canonize man's own progress. His hope is rather a hope against every hope which we place in the man-made idols of our secular society. The Christian hope is not a cunning trick of man's reason in order to unravel the mysteries (*Entmysterialisierung*) of the future. Christian eschatology is not an omniscient ideology about the future, but a *theologia negativa* of the future. This poverty of knowledge is rather the very wealth of Christianity. What distinguishes the Christian and the secular ideologies of the future from one another is not that the Christians know *more*, but that they know *less* about the sought-after future of humanity and that they face up to this poverty of knowledge: "By faith Abraham obeyed when he was called to go out to a place which he was to receive as an inheritance; and he went out not knowing where he was to go" (cf. Heb. 11, 8). Moreover, the Christian hope is aware of its own fatal perils; in short, it is aware of death. For in the face of death all shining promises fade away. This Christian hope is the anticipatory (proleptic) practice in dying. And even this aspect of hope should not be limited to an individualistic and worldless attitude. Christian hope is essentially directed to the world of our brother, since this hope fulfills itself in love for the other, for the least of our brothers. Only in this kenosis of love is death overcome. "We know that we have passed out of death into life, because we love the brethren" (cf. I Jn. 3,14). The Christian hope enters into the passion of death in this kenosis of love to the least of our brothers. This is the imitation of Jesus: He did not live for himself, but for us. Hope is this living for "the other."

NOTES

1 Cf. K. Rahner, "Theology and Anthropology," p. 23, footnote 1.

2 Gerhard Ebeling, *Wort und Glaube,* Tubingen, J. C. B. Mohr (Paul Siebeck), 1062, 387.

3 Cf. Johanes B. Metz, "Zukunft des Glaubens in einer hominisierten Welt," in *Weltverständnis im Glauben,* edited by Johannes Metz, Matthias-Grünewald, Mainz, 1965, 45–62.

4 Cf. Francis Fiorenza, "Säkularisation und die säkularisierte Stadt," *Stimmen der Zeit,* Mai, 1966.

5 Cf. Johannes B. Metz, "Gott vor uns," *Ernst Bloch zu Ehren,* Frankfort, Suhrkamp Verlag, 1965, 227–241.

6 Cf. Johannes B. Metz, Welt, *LThK,* X, 1023–1026.

7 Cf. Wolfhart Pannenberg, "Der Gott der Hoffnung," in *Ernst Bloch zu Ehren, op. cit.,* 215.

8 *Ibid.,* 212.

9 Cf. Karl Rahner, "Kirche und Parusie Christi," *Schriften zur Theologie,* Einsiedeln, Benziger Verlag, 1965, 351.

10 Cf. Jürgen Moltmann, *Theologie der Hoffnung,* Munchen, Ch. Kaiser Verlag, 1964, 2nd edition, 304.

11 *Ibid.,* 303.

JEAN DANIELOU

Christianity and
non-Christian Religions

An invitation to consider the nature of non-Christian religions
and their relationship to Christian revelation has been given to
us through the establishment of the Secretariat for Non-Christian
Religions, and through the call for dialogue with all religious
bodies sounded in the Encyclical *Ecclesiam Suam* as well as in
the Declaration on Non-Christian Religions. A preliminary statement clarifying our position on this subject is necessary if we
are to avoid the extremes both of syncretism, which classifies
Christianity as simply part of the general phenomenon of religion, while granting its preeminence, and sectarianism, which
fails to recognize positive content in non-Christian religions.
This subject is important today from the standpoint of presen-
ting the Christian message, of establishing dialogue and coopera-
tion with non-Christians and also of enabling us to discern pagan
elements in Christianity.

I intend to limit my consideration to the sphere of pagan
religions, and by "pagan religions" I mean those religions which
are beyond the context of historical revelation. Consequently,
I shall not consider the question of Judaism which is a quite
special case with its Judaeo-Christian borrowings. Furthermore,
I do not intend to consider the non-religious world, which is

sometimes designated incorrectly by the term "pagan." The pagan is essentially the religious *man*, and nothing is more opposed to paganism than atheism.

The non-Christian religions express one dimension of human nature. Man is fundamentally religious, that is, capable of recognizing by intelligence and of ratifying by love his relation to the Divinity. This is true historically since religious rites along with tools are considered by the ethnologist as signs of the advent of man. It is true for the psychologist who recognizes in the depths of man a dimension irreducible to other spheres of experience. It is especially true for a sound philosophy which recognizes humanism as authentic only when it depicts man in his threefold dimension: his mastery of the universe through technology, his communion with others through love, and his conversion towards God through adoration.

In this sense, the religious act does not refer exclusively to another world. It is basic to this world. One of the aberrations of contemporary secularism is to think that a humanism can be formulated without it. A world without God is an inhuman world. God is part of civilization. This is true on an individual level, since love of God is a condition for man's complete fulfillment, for his happiness; and it is also true on a collective level since the religious act is part of the temporal common good. I am speaking of the religious act regardless of the forms used for its expression.

Numerous attempts have been made to give the religious act a positivistic explanation: *cosmological*—the mystery of nature, which is simply the as yet unexplained; *psychological*—the sublimation of instinctive life, especially of *eros; sociological*—transcendence is simply the expression of the submission of an individual to familial and national collectivity. All of these explanations come from detailed facts which are incorrectly interpreted. The signs through which the sacred is manifested are confused with its very substance.

It is in fact the distinctive characteristic of religions, that they perceive the divine through its manifestations. Mircea Eliade calls these manifestations "hierophanies." They can be classified in several ways. They may be cosmic phenomena: a starry sky, a storm with lightning and thunder, a crag—unyielding, unchangeable, majestic; a serpent, tranquil water, and the moon to convey the mystery of fertility. All these are signs through which men of all times have perceived a divine presence. When a young sophisticate ridicules an old woman for making the sign of the cross during a storm, it is not necessary to ask which one is intelligent!

The presence of the sacred is even more strongly perceived through human actions. Sacralization of the principal stages of human existence is one of the most fundamental traits of all religions. The birth of a child, the beginning of adolescence, marriage, and death are always accompanied by religious rites. The seasonal rhythm of work is celebrated in a liturgical cycle. Human deeds reproduce the model deeds performed by the gods in the world of archetypes. Thus rites and myths express a fundamental experience by which man touches a world which transcends him.

Positivistic explanations of religion err in attempting to identify what is essentially a sign with the very substance of religion. Eliade and van der Leeuw have rightly observed that is was not the sun as a material object which the disciples of Mithra adored, but through the sun they adored the beneficent power which is the source of light and of life. And if religion is expressed through social structures, as Levi-Strauss has correctly pointed out, this is not because it is reducible to those structures: rather, through basic human relationships man rejoins a reality which he cannot control and which places him in the presence of the transcendent.

Finally, in experiencing at the same time both his own limits and that in himself which is absolute, man perceives the presence of a divine reality in his inner self, distinct from himself, yet acting within him. Man perceives this reality in the restraints of his conscience making him aware of absolute good and evil; he perceives it in the enlightenment of his mind bringing him into contact with a truth dwelling at the heart of his being; he perceives it in the summons of a love making him search beyond all that is finite for that Good which makes every good thing truly good. When retreating within himself to the depths of his personal life, a man is sometimes dazzled, in a sense, by perceiving a ray coming from some other source, but held fast in the mirror of his own soul.

The realm of religion is one of the privileged areas of human experience. Although enriched by scientific discoveries and the creative developments of society, human experience can find no better vehicle for expressing its most intimate content than religion. The great religions are the historical expression of the religious act in mankind. The great religions are, at the same time, both one and diverse. They are one, because they correspond to the same level of experience: in its own fashion, each one makes us aware of the ways in which men have recognized God through the world and sought Him beyond the world.

At the same time, diversity is part of the essence of the great religions. Each one is the expression of the peculiar religious genius of a people. In fact, nothing characterizes a people better than their religion. In this context, the old axiom *cujus regio, ejus religio* is quite accurate. Religion forms part of the heritage of a people. And if religion is the characteristic expression of a race's religious genius, a man can no more change his religion than he could change his race. Religions are one of creation's most remarkable aspects and contribute to its splendor. How, then, could Christianity destroy these religions? Christianity with its mission not to destroy but to fulfill, to save what has been created? To become a Christian is not to change one's religion but to move from the plane of religion to that of truth. Each race does this in its own way.

In this sense, nothing could be more false than to identify Christianity as the religion of the west. It belongs to an entirely different order. There is a religion of the west, and this religion is ancient paganism: Greek or Latin, Celtic or Germanic. This religion is equivalent to modern Hinduism or Taoism, animism or the religions of the American Indians. Shankara can be compared to Plotinus, Confucius to Socrates. This form of paganism is as valid as the others. It is not too distant from us, for we are really only converted pagans. *"Fiunt, non nascuntur Christiani,"* said Tertullian, and we might translate that statement to read, "One is born a pagan, one becomes a Christian." This religious genius of the west colors the western way of being a Christian. We have the duty to be faithful to this western way but not to impose it on others.

There are various types of pagan soul, each with its own beauty. All deserve to be saved and all, indeed, can be saved. The pagan soul of the Semites was the first to be saved, in Abraham. Then followed the pagan soul of the west: the so-called baptism of Plato and Virgil. Perhaps in the twentieth century it will be the pagan soul of Africa, and in the twenty-first century the pagan soul of India. The differences in Christianity reflect, in the unity of one faith which is necessarily one, the different types of religious mentality which welcome this faith, each in its own way. What right have I to force on others my way of welcoming Jesus Christ?

Specifying these relationships between Christianity and other religions is clearly essential for establishing dialogue on a firm basis. In this matter, as in ecumenical affairs, love must be accompanied by clarity, for nothing can be based on confusion. Syncretism errs in putting everything on the same plane, thus making dialogue superfluous. But there is an equivalent error which grows out of sentimental attitudes that avoid a clear statement of basic issues for fear of creating barriers. Clarification of the problem is necessary.

We have given a description of the religious fact in general. The Judaeo-Christian fact presents us with something quite different. It is not simply a collection of resources for worshipping God. It is testimony to an event, an event which constitutes sacred history. The sacred book of the Christians is a history, bearing witness to God's actions, to the Word's invasion of history. It is not necessary to be a Christian to believe in God, but it is necessary to be one to believe that God came among men. Religions are a movement of man toward God; revelation testifies to a movement of God towards man.

The antithetical results of this fact are obvious. The object of all religions is to manifest God through the repetition of natural and human cycles. The object of revelation is a unique event, designated as *hapax* in the Epistle to the Hebrews. If this event is unique, revelation must necessarily be unique. It consists in believing in the reality of that unique event. Religions on the other hand are normally diverse. Created by human genius, they testify to the worth of important religious figures —Buddha, Zoroaster, Orpheus,—but they are marked by the defects of human production. Revelation is the work of God alone. Man can lay no claim to it for it does not belong to him. It is a pure gift. By that very fact it is infallible: true, in a sense which applies to God alone.

Religion is mainly concerned with the present life. It is one aspect of natural human existence; it is the continuum of lasting values. Revelation is eschatological, concerned with the last things which are beyond man's grasp. It is turned towards the future; it is prophetic. Religion expresses man's desire for God. Revelation testifies that God has responded to this desire. Religion does not provide salvation. Jesus Christ alone grants salvation. Again, revelation does not destroy religion but fulfills it.

Religion is the domain of spiritual experience. It is man's effort to develop that part of himself which is turned towards the divine. Consequently, a religion's value will vary in proportion to the spiritual endowments of its adherents. Revelation on the other hand is the domain of faith. It is not based on personal experience: rather, it asks man to entrust himself to the experience of another, one who came from on high and was born in glory. Since then, revelation is offered to the poor. Faith alone is important, along with the grace which operates in human weakness.

Thus, if there is opposition between Christianity and other religions, this opposition does not represent incompatible realities in the same category: rather, this opposition signifies a connection between the two. If there is danger in syncretism, there is an equal danger in a radicalism which, in the name of faith, fails to acknowledge the religious act and its importance. Such an attitude is very widespread today. It makes the destruction of religion a condition for faith, and it is violently opposed to the elements of paganism remaining in Christianity. It rates atheism's destruction of religion as a preparation for faith.

It seems that the encyclical *Ecclesiam Suam* reacts successfully against such an attitude. While it rejects atheism as a perversion of human nature, the encyclical directs a fraternal appeal to non-biblical religions, thus attesting both to their vitality in the world and to the values which they continue to preserve. Pius XII's encyclical *Evangelii Praecones* is especially important since it gave an admirable description of Christianity's attitude toward pagan religious values by saying that Christianity assumed these values, purified them, and transfigured them. These three features are most important.

First of all, Christianity assumes pagan religious values and does not destroy them. This is true theologically since Christ, as we have said, came to take hold of every man, and the most valuable man is the religious man. It is also true historically. Although Christianity always starts to identify itself in a pagan country by opposing the errors of paganism, later on it takes over the valuable elements of paganism. The evangelization of the west provides clear proof of this process. Christianity recovered all the values of Greek and Roman religions. The Virgin Mary replaced pagan goddesses in the temples. Christmas and Candlemas replaced the rhythm of pagan festivals.

Another aspect of this Christian assumption of that which is pagan through revelation concerns its diverse expressions. We have said that the religious genius of races is different and that Christianity must assume this peculiar genius in all its diversity. However, until now only the western world has been evangelized in both its culture and its religious spirit, and the Christianity which the western world has spread has been a western Christianity.

Here we touch upon basic problems. A distinct trait of our present situation is the rejection of Christianity by races in the Far East and the Near East in the name of their own religion. We must admit that this reaction is justified insofar as the Christian revelation presented to them is identified with the type of Christianity practiced in the west. What they rightly refuse is not Christianity but the western form of Christianity. This is a case of effectively destroying the cultural values to which these races have a right and a duty to be attached.

One difficulty might be properly introduced at this point. Is not the view we have given of paganism overly optimistic? Is the relationship of pagan elements to Christianity only one of assumption? Does not one imply a break with the other? Such questions are quite justified. If we take the religious act in its theoretical reality, it is one aspect of creation, and thus it is good. But this act as it has, in fact, been expressed in historical religions is always more or less deformed. Man's religions, like all man's affairs, belong to a world marked by sin and they bear its traces. In this sense they are stumbling blocks at the same time that they are stepping stones.

The second service which revelation renders to religion has

bearing on this aspect of the question. Revelation purifies paganism. It is the invisible God whom pagan man adores through visible realities, but his adoration often stops at the visible realities and then degenerates into idolatry. St. Paul teaches this in the opening section of his *Epistle to the Romans:* "From the foundations of the world men have caught sight of his invisible nature, his eternal power, and his divineness, as they are known through his creatures . . . and they exchanged the glory of the imperishable God for representations of perishable man, of bird and beast and reptile" (Rom. I:20, 23).

It is certainly a fact that pagan religions appear to be filled with disturbing and sinister elements. Sometimes it seems that they are privileged domains of the forces of evil. The Fathers of the Church were not entirely wrong in recognizing demoniac forces at work, seeking to divert towards themselves the natural movement of man's heart towards God. Religious rites are degraded by magic and reduced to serving human passions; superstition substitutes for prayer, desire for the unusual replaces the sense of mystery. Extraordinary perversions, consecrated prostitution, sacrifices of children, sexual mutilations—all these flow, as St. Paul observed, from a perversion of the spirit.

On a higher level, the most profound searchings of the religions remain tentative. The lines dividing the divine and the created are never traced clearly. The greatest minds did not emerge from a pantheism which dissolves the divine in the universe, and fails to arrive at the idea of a transcendent and personal God. Spiritual experience becomes an end in itself: even in this experience man stops short at himself, and his most sublime dimension becomes an object of self-adoration. The mystery of evil becomes, so to speak, dislocated. It is thought of either as a burden which man must overcome, or as a negative pole of being, eternally opposed to the good in a terrifying dialectic.

Thus, on the level of religion itself, Christianity makes its influence felt. Of course we know full well that Christianity is located on another plane. We have shown this by describing its specific nature. Nevertheless, even on this level, Christianity shows a relationship with pagan religious values: it transfigures them. The salvation brought by Christ does not consist in substituting another reality for that of nature. It is man, his own creature, that the Word comes to save, and the man he has created is a religious man. Thus the Word has come to transfigure religious values as well.

It is easy to demonstrate this transfiguration on the different planes where the religious act is found. On all these planes the life of the Holy Spirit comes to take possession of the religious man to lead him into the very life of God. The pagan man searches for God through the natural signs which manifest divinity; that is to say, he is separated from God by His infinite transcendence. Man cannot cross the abyss of transcendence, but God can. He searches for man, puny though he is, and raises him up to Himself, drawing him into intimacy with Himself, that is, into the very life of the Holy Trinity.

But this man who is drawn into the intimacy of God's life is the same one who sought God through signs. And these same signs—these "hierophanies"—which succeeded in revealing the spiritual life exteriorly now serve to express it interiorly. If fire expressed God's purifying power, water, his unifying strength, and breath, his creative power, all these images can now designate the actions of divine persons. The Spirit is the fire which Christ came to kindle on earth, the divine breath which aroused the Apostles, the living water which gushed forth from the throne of God and the Lamb.

If man's religious acts have been the point of insertion of the sacred, those same acts now signify the fulfillment of the longing they awakened. This involves a new birth, not of the flesh but of the spirit, giving rise to a life which is the incorruptible life of God and not the frail life of the flesh. It involves nuptials which are a participation in the marriage of the Word and humanity, which introduce the soul to the participation of divine goods. It involves death, which is no longer a separation of soul and body but a shedding of mortal life in order to rise again with Christ.

Interior experience, moveover, is part of that human nature which is caught up by grace. Of course, if this experience pretends to be sufficient in itself, especially if it considers itself superior to faith, it becomes the supreme temptation. By contrast, however, if this experience opens itself to grace, it will attain supreme fulfillment. But if, as Father de Lubac has said, mystery does not become mystique, if it does not become internalized, then it will remain on the level of merely exterior faith and formal practice.

This last remark leads us to two important pastoral questions. We have just said that the relationship of Christianity and paganism is reciprocal. Christianity is necessary for revelation to be fulfilled, but the actual quality of this fulfillment depends upon the quality of the religious man transformed by revelation. Consequently, Christianity needs a natural religion, just as it needs all human realities since its sole mission is to redeem what has first been created.

And there we confront the problem of the sacred in the contemporary world. If grace comes to take possession of the man who is already religious, what will happen when man is no longer religious, when he has lost the sense of the sacred? How can light become the symbol of the sun of justice rising in the east to illuminate a new creation when the sun has ceased to be a hierophany and is thought to be nothing more than a colossal atomic explosion?

How can a meal become a sign and a sacrament of the Christians' communion with Christ and each other when it has lost the dignity and sacredness which it once had, when it merely satisfies an instinct and is no longer a human activity expressing communion? How can human love, profaned by eroticism and drained of its sacredness and mystery, still be a symbol of the love of Christ and the Church? How can death, robbed by euthanasia of its meaning as a personal act of total abandonment to God, still signify a transition to truly genuine life?

Only meaningful things can be transfigured. Let us attempt to answer only one question. The dialogue of revelation with the pagan world traverses the problem of religion and atheism, namely, the problem of the religious man. Revelation, in fact, suffers less than religion in today's world, but those who think that revelation can get along without religion are mistaken. This is the error of Bonhoeffer and Tillich, and also of Robinson, who repeats their question. When directed to man without God, revelation means nothing more than human activity. Jeanson is right, then, in inviting Christians to free Christianity from the burden of God, to free revelation from religion.

But the problem has been poorly stated, its distinguishing features have not been clarified. The problem is not whether revelation can get along without the sacred: rather, the problem is to know the points of contact with the sacred—better still, since the points of contact with the sacred are the same, the problem is to know how we can express in the language of today what we continue too often to express in the language of yesterday. We are prisoners of words, we do not come to grips with the things themselves.

The sacred, indeed, is always there, but we do not know how to recognize it, and for that reason, we no longer recognize the religious man whom faith must reach in order to save. It is not in the rear guard of traditionalism that one finds the sacred in the world today, but in the forefront of living research. Strangely enough, we find the sacred where it has always been, but where today's world will discover it only through a fresh and vital encounter. As Father Teilhard saw, it is in mankind on the march that the need for worship comes to life again. The sacred rises once more in the world of nature precisely to the extent that science attains new dimensions. The sun again becomes a sacred sign precisely to the extent that it is discovered to be a colossal atomic explosion, charged with all the terror that these words suggest to men who feel this frail planet is threatened. Modern man rediscovers the sacred in the depths of space and time; better images of the infinite than the very limited cosmos which aroused religious sentiment in ancient man. Furthermore, it is on the level of human activity that technology, in reaching its limits, clashes with a world that it cannot master, and returns to the mystery of God through the mystery of man, the image of God. When technology attempts to penetrate the deepest human realities and touches on the laws of life's transmission, it encounters an element in human love which stems from the mystery of the community of persons, an element which cannot be reduced to eugenic or demographic principles. When technology encounters death it feels totally inadequate, for it has no answer to explain death's personal meaning, which involves, of course, the ultimate destiny of man.

The problem of tomorrow is not the problem of atheism. It is the problem of a new paganism which is in search of itself. It is this new source of dialogue that the Church is actually seeking as she listens to the voice of this age and attempts to interpret the signs of the times. For it is through the signs of the times that God speaks, in human nature. Atheism is only a transition from the paganism of yesterday—that of rural civilization—to the paganism of tomorrow—that of industrial civilization. The paganism of tomorrow is the religious issue for modern man. It is this issue which the Church must address, for that is what she must assume, purify, and transfigure if it is to remain true that a Christian is nothing more than a pagan on the way to conversion.

This brings us to the second question which concerns the

presence of pagan elements in Christianity. That there should be pagan elements in Christianity ought not to surprise us. We have seen that Christianity needs pagan man in order to save him. Equally, there never are any Christians in an absolute sense; there are only pagans in various degrees of conversion. However, it can and often does happen that the distinctly Christian element in Christianity is ultimately diminished and the pagan element predominates.

It is a fact that many Christians live Christianity not so much according to that which constitutes its specific content, but more according to their own way of being a pagan, that is, they live Christianity as a religion. Because they are born in Christian countries, they fulfill by means of Christian rites the human need of consecrating the principal acts of human life—birth, marriage, death. This paganism is superior to other forms because it is a purified paganism but we must recognize the fact that often it is nothing more than paganism lacking specifically Christian faith.

However, should this type of Christianity be condemned? In a world threatened by atheism the substance of the sacred must be defended wherever it is found. The fact that men are not content to dissociate God from the principal acts of their lives is an indication of a religious base which provides the soil where faith can grow. Furthermore, Christianity demands a personal approach. It is quite normal that in a Christian country many first live Christianity as religion before they really discover it as revelation.

Tension between paganism and Christianity is completely normal. As we have seen, it exists not only between Christianity and non-Christian religions, but it also exists between Christianity as revelation and Christianity as religion, between a personal Christianity and a sociological Christianity, between a Christianity of commitment and Christianity of practice. It would be a serious mistake to fail to recognize the importance of this tension, to eliminate from Christianity all that is not personal commitment, to scorn sociological Christianity. Such a mistake would abandon to atheism an entire people who find in Christianity a means of satisfying their natural need for God in a most innocent form, a people who find available in Christianity the seed of revelation which will thrive in some of them.

We have said that Christianity does not consist in knowing God; religion is sufficient for that. But, in point of fact, without Christianity other religions do not know the true God, or, better still, they do not truly know God. It is a tremendous thing to know God truly. It is the fulfillment of the nature of man himself, the foundation of his morality, the heart of his society. The Church has always affirmed that its mission was not only to bring the light of Christ to bear on man's supernatural and eschatological destiny but also to illuminate man's natural life, providing for him the conditions of his earthly happiness. That is something we must not forget.

From this point of view one may speak of Christian religion as one speaks of Christian philosophy, Christian civilization, Christian customs. Not that Christianity can be merely a philosophy, a civilization, a religion, or a type of humanism of however high a level. This would be a completely mistaken interpretation. Christianity is more than that: it is a salvific action of God. But it also allows human realities to discover their fullness, even before introducing the transfiguration which makes them surpass themselves. In this sense Christianity exerts an influence on religion by helping it become pure and free from darkness.

But it is also true that in the very heart of Christianity the religious element is liable to be degraded. Thus there is a problem not of purifying Christianity of its religious element, but of purifying this religious element itself. Many elements of popular piety—devotion to the Blessed Virgin and the saints, processions and pilgrimages, blessings and exorcisms, medals and scapulars, candles and votive offerings—enhance a religious element which has its place in Christianity and which the Church has always defended against those who would like to eliminate it. Nevertheless, these religious elements can easily degenerate into superstition, and thus they are continually in need of being purified.

From these remarks we may draw a conclusion about the attention which Christianity must give to paganism. On the one hand, the problem is complex and involves traditional pagan religions, the neo-paganism of industrial civilization, and even paganism within the Church. On the other hand, there is the value of paganism. Taken as a natural religion, paganism seems to be a dimension of humanism. By that token paganism is an element of the temporal common good, at the same time that it presents to Christianity that which Christianity is called to save. Paganism gives Christianity its points of contact with non-Christian religions and with the needs of the contemporary world. By beginning with paganism and its orientation towards Christianity, a truly Christian people is made possible. A false conception of the purity of revelation in relation to paganism would contradict the spirit of the mystery of the Incarnation.

GEORGE A. LINDBECK

The Framework of Catholic-
Protestant Disagreement

It was, I believe, Talleyrand who once remarked that the French
and Austrians fought over Venice, not because they disagreed,
but because they agreed: they both wanted it. If only the common framework, the presuppositions, of their national policies
had been different, there would have been no war.

The analogy is by no means perfect, but still, something similar is true of Roman Catholic-Protestant disagreements. The disputes which raged in the sixteenth century were in part depend-
ent on a common theological framework. That framework is
now in the process of changing. All of us, Protestants and
Roman Catholics alike, increasingly experience and interpret
both natural and supernatural realities in categories very different from those of the past. With this, some of our classic
differences are disappearing and new ones which do not always
follow the old boundaries between the confessions, are arising.
This is not because either side has surrendered its traditional
positions, but because these are now more and more formulated
in such ways that they often no longer seem incompatible, or at
least not incompatible in the old ways.

I would like, first, to recall some examples of what many
people think of as disappearing conflicts, then characterize the

new framework, describe one divergence which develops within it, and, finally, say a few words about the changes which some of the old disagreements undergo within the new framework.

Our attention will be largely limited to theological issues in the narrower sense of the term. Very little will be said about the radical newness of the sociological, cultural and political world situation in which the churches find themselves. This concrete setting of the churches is a major contributing cause to the theological developments which we shall discuss. But we must, for the sake of brevity and clarity, abstract from this problem of the relation of the church and world, even though it is the fundamental and all-encompassing one, and focus on a selection of the issues which it has helped to engender. Even so, our treatment will necessarily be sketchy.

I

We are all to some degree aware that increasing numbers of Catholics and Protestants consider many of the major disputes of the past obsolescent. We have heard rumors, for example, that Karl Barth's version of the Reformation doctrine of justification is regarded by Hans Küng as good Catholic teaching. We have heard that Karl Rahner doubts that Trent's affirmation of transubstantiation differs basically from what many Lutherans (and, we should add, many other Protestants) understand by the real presence. In reference to the sacrifice of the Mass, which many sixteenth century Protestants considered the worst of Catholic errors, something like agreement across inter-confessional lines is now developing in certain circles. When we come to scripture and tradition, we discover that some Catholics now like to use the phrase, *sola scriptura,* even if they do add *in ore ecclesiae,* while a largely Protestant drafting group, of which I happened to be a member, proposed the formula, *sola traditione,* at the Faith and Order Conference of the World Council of

Churches in Montreal in 1963. More and more our disagreements seem to center on or derive from the doctrine of the church, and even here many theologians on both sides are thinking in common categories which make our differences seem like variations on common themes rather than the totally discordant compositions they once appeared to be.

I myself am becoming more and more skeptical of the possibility of finding one or two divergences from which all others flow. The *sola fide* and the *sola scriptura,* which so well summed up the differences at the time of the Reformation, no longer serve this purpose. Paul Tillich's effort to discover the heart of the matter in the Protestant principle—the principle that nothing finite is to be absolutized—seems less and less applicable in view of the growing awareness, on the Catholic side, that the church is *semper reformada,* and the complementary recognition in many Protestant circles that, as Tillich himself acknowledged, Catholic substance is indispensible. The Catholic theologian, Van de Pol, has tried to mark the watershed by contrasting revelation as word with revelation as reality, and Congar has made a somewhat similar distinction in Christological terms, but there are thoroughly Protestant theologians who insist on the need for ontology, and Catholics who see nothing wrong with making the Word systematically central if this is properly done.

It is possible to go even farther. There are indications that we are moving into an era when we shall find similarly structured theological systems on both sides of the confessional divide. A Protestant dogmatician who follows the French Protestant exegete, Cullman, will pattern his dogmatics on *Heilsgeschichte,* the history of salvation, but so also does the Catholic Swiss theologian, Johannes Feiner. If Hans Küng had written a dogmatics a few years ago—or perhaps even now—it probably would be Barthian in structure; and I myself see no impossibility in constructing a Protestant systematic theology which is basically Rahnerian in outline.

Actually this kind of interchange is already common in ecumenical discussions. We find instances of Protestant and Catholic participants who use similar systematic principles, starting points and methods. This does not mean, to be sure, that their dogmatic disagreements disappear, but these disagreements, in some cases, become, so to speak, exceptional. Over ninety per cent or more of the dogmatic cycle, they say much the same things in much the same ways; but then they push and pull their similar theological constructions in order to reach different conclusions on a relatively small number of points, the Catholic, for example, affirming a certain kind of magisterial authority which the Protestant excludes. This is still largely confined to men whose entire thinking has been influenced by the ecumenical dialogue, but it seems likely to continue to develop rapidly and increasingly influence ordinary dogmatic writing even when this is done without any formally ecumenical purpose.

As I have already said, not only does the changed framework of theological discussion lead to the reconciliation of old differences, but it can also occasion the emergence of new ones. We shall later have a good deal to say about the dispute over extreme existentialism as an example of this. However, it is important to remember that such a conflict is not between Protestants and Catholics as such, but rather cuts across confessional boundaries. Some Catholics, Gotthold Hasenhüttl, for instance, are a good deal more sympathetic to the existentialism of Rudolph Bultmann than are large numbers of Protestants; and the opponents of extreme existentialism, in turn, whether Protestant or Catholic, often formulate their objections in very similar terms.

II

What, then, are the characteristics of this contemporary framework of thought which lead to the reshuffling of the theological lines? It would be presumptuous to pretend that any brief description such as I shall offer is adequate. It may miss the really salient features, and it will certainly be incomplete. But my purpose is primarily to stimulate thinking about the changing context of our disagreements and about how this affects ecumenical discussions. This, I hope, even an inadequate analysis can do.

I find myself agreeing with those who suggest that, at least as far as theology is concerned, the greatest difference between our outlook and that of the 16th century is that we are vastly more aware, both experientially and reflectively, of the historical dimensions of reality, both human and non-human. The relatively static, classical two-story world picture is finally disappearing. It began influencing Christian thought in the Patristic period, became fully articulated and dominant in Christianized versions during the middle ages, and persisted in both Protestantism and Catholicism long into what is called modern times. Indeed, it did not become theologically untenable until after the growth of historical knowledge and evolutionary theories in the nineteenth century and the demolition of the static, non-historical world of Newtonian physics which was not completed until the 20th. Some observers would be inclined to see the influence of this traditional framework as still visible in the thought of contemporary giants such as Paul Tillich or Karl Barth. Be that as it may, the present-day theologian knows himself to be set in a universe whose temporal dimensions are unimaginably greater than those of the 16th century. The cosmic epoch in which we live commenced, not six thousand years ago, but considerably more than six billion years in the past, and will go on, so the most recent rumors from the astrophysicists indicate, either indefinitely or 70 odd billion years longer. Much more important than mere temporal duration, however, is that we picture the world as a unified, developing process in which the past is not at all like the present, nor the present like the future. Life came after ages of stellar evolution in which this earth, at least, was lifeless. Amoebas were followed after 600 million years by man, and the descendents of the first primitive cave dwellers after some hundreds of thousands of years have turned into astronauts reaching for the stars.

Now the picture that we paint of this developing universe is not as optimistically progressive as it often was a generation or two ago. It has acquired apocalyptic features even in the eyes of many non-Christians. The corruption of the best is the worst, so every advance, however genuinely wonderful, brings with it the possibility of ever greater catastrophes. As a consequence, we cannot contrast our outlook with that of the sixteenth century in terms of optimism and pessimism or belief and disbelief in progress. The difference is more radical. We no longer share the assumption of 400 years ago that the basic structures of the physical world, of human life and of religious existence have been and always will be much the same until the end of time. The world of human beings is changing with ever-accelerating rapidity, not as a matter of sheer flux, but in a definite direction whose final end is both fascinating and terrifying, for it seems to offer the possibility of unimaginable achievements and unimaginable disasters, and is in any case beyond the possibility of empirical prediction.

The religious implications of this are immense. Put over-simply, that which transcends the reality which we experience and know is no longer thought of (as it was in a two-story, non-historical universe) as a realm of timeless truth, value and being above us (or, where the immanence of the divine is emphasized, within and at the ground of being) which supplies the permanently stable structures of life. Rather, that which transcends the world of our experience lies ahead, in the undecipherable possibilities for good and evil into which we find ourselves hurled with ever-increasing speed. Our contemporaries are not likely to encounter transcendence as something discontinuous with the world, as something which is to be entered by escaping out of time into eternity. Rather, they meet it as the future which is continuous, yet radically different, from our present world; they encounter it within the reality of their experience as the anticipations or projections of the coming world.

This is the specifically modern experience of transcendence, but, of course, vast numbers of our contemporaries do not seem to have it, or at least do not consciously articulate it. We are all aware of the snow-balling secularization and the practical, even when not theoretical, atheism of present-day thinking and feeling. The sense of transcendence appropriate to a two-story outlook is vanishing, and with it the relevance of theological constructions and modes of piety which developed within that framework. This presumably is the kernel of truth contained within the distortions of the God-is-dead theologies. It is indeed true that our awareness of the historicity of the cosmos and of human existence is destroying many of the ideas which Christians have often substituted for the living God of our Lord Jesus Christ and of Abraham, Isaac and Jacob.

When our situation is looked at in these terms, then the fundamental theological response to the new problematic is to be seen in the revival of biblical eschatological thinking. If the analysis we have suggested is substantially correct, then it is to this that the theological future belongs. To be sure, this revival has in part been prompted by modern scholarly research, itself correlated with the historical perspective, which has made clear how radically unbiblical was the classical framework of nearly two thousand years of Christian thought. But biblical eschatology, as we all know, is not gaining ground only because theologians think they should be faithful to the scriptural witness, even though this, fortunately, does play an important part. Its success, however, is to be attributed mostly to the fact that the eschatology of the New Testament makes sense in the modern framework in a way that it did not in the classical outlook. As a consequence, it no longer needs to be banished to a kind of post-script in the theological manuals and in Christian spirituality. It can move once again into the center, so that hope, anticipation and openness for the future salvation which God is preparing for the world as a whole can once again become an essential dimension and mainspring of Christian faith and love.

It is, then, this revival of biblical eschatology in conjunction with the modern sense of the historical character of existence which, I am suggesting, provides the new framework, the common framework, for both the Protestant and Catholic theology which is likely to be important for the churches during the coming period.

III

We have mentioned that an alteration in framework both changes past problems and generates new ones. Let us start with illustrating the new problems by describing two divergent contemporary ways of appropriating biblical eschatology which I shall call, for lack of better terms, the "objectivist" and the "non-objectivist." We shall then turn, in the last section of this study, to some indication of what happens to the old Catholic-Protestant controversies when these are viewed within the objectivist version of eschatology.

It is, in a way, very misleading to contrast "objectivist" with "non-objectivist" because, within the eschatological-historical framework, neither of these terms mean the same as in traditional contexts. Both of these positions agree in emphasizing the existential and personal dimensions of faith. It is hard, indeed, to imagine any authentic recovery of biblical eschatology which fails to do this. The New Testament stresses that the whole man to the very depths of his being is confronted with the necessity to decide for or against the future, for or against the New Age which has begun in Christ and will be consummated at his return. The cry, "Repent, for the Kingdom of God is at hand," stands at the very center of the gospel. However, those whom I am calling non-objectivists, even when they are not formally and self-consciously existentialists, tend to exclude everything except this personal-existential emphasis. They tend to ignore or demythologize the objective cosmic images through which the biblical writers expressed their faith and hope in God's realistically future transformation of this world, the concrete world in which we live, into a new heaven and new earth.

The objectivists, in contrast, retain these themes, and are interested in trying to show how through them one can give a genuinely Christian, a genuinely biblical, interpretation of the modern historical-developmental world view. This world, they sugggest, in its very physical reality will be transformed in the Kingdom of God which has begun in Jesus Christ. All that is pure, honorable and of good report, whether it develops within the explicitly Christian sphere or not, whether it is specifically religious or apparently secular in character, will enter into the final consummation. We are all somewhat familiar, I suppose, with the ways in which some versions of this view insist that genuine human advances of all sorts, therefore, have eternal value: the course of earthly history and the worldly tasks which necessarily occupy the attention of most men most of the time are not simply a meaningless background to spiritual realities, but enter into their very constitution.

This is not at all the same as an immanentism which substitutes evolution, creative or otherwise, for God. The final manifestation of the Kingdom will not be an earthly achievement; it will burst disjunctively into history from above just as it began in Jesus Christ, not as an emergent novelty, but as God's transcendent act. Yet, according to this application of eschatology to the modern world view, God is now guiding all the processes of nature and history in preparation for the fulfillment, just as all history before Christ was preparation for Him who came in the fullness of time and as the fulfillment of all times.

This end of history cannot, of course, be imagined or described. It can be represented only in pictures or symbols whether these be those of the Apocalypse of Saint John or, in our day, the perhaps equally nonliteral scientific imaginings of a Teilhard de Chardin. Yet that end and that fulfillment is real. The statements which assert it are affirmed in faith to be propositionally true in the empirically, even though eschatologically, verifiable sense which modern analytic philosophy makes a condition for meaningful speech.

The approach which I am trying to describe has not yet been comprehensively formulated, but the beginnings of it are everywhere in evidence. I myself first became clearly aware of it as a possible theological option in the work of Karl Rahner, but it is now to be found incipiently in passage after passage in the conciliar documents, especially in the Constitution on the Church in the Modern World.

It has, I think it must be admitted, more affinities with traditional Catholic emphasis than with Protestant ones, simply because it does not confine itself to personalistic and existentialist categories, but also makes use of objective, ontological constructions. It can be stated in terms which make it seem a historicized version of, for example, such assertions as that grace does not destroy, but perfects nature, and the soul is the form of the body. It can be presented, even if not always very plausibly, as basically a kind of Thomistic position suitably reinterpreted in the context of a modern historical, rather than a static Aristotelian, world view.

Nevertheless, it is fundamentally different from the 16th century scholasticism to which the Reformers objected, and consequently the old criticisms simply do not apply. It represents a kind of approach which Protestants can adopt and, indeed, under the impact of modern developments, a number of them are working independently along parallel lines. Examples of such thinkers are the younger German theologians, Wolfhart Pannenberg and, more especially, Jürgen Moltmann.

However, it is probably true that most Protestants are sharply opposed to this kind of objective eschatology and prefer versions which, even if not formally existential, are more exclusively concerned with the present and personal reality of the Eschaton. In part, no doubt, this is because Protestant theologians have painful memories of the evolutionary optimism of the 19th century liberalism and consequently are intensely suspicious of efforts to relate the concrete social, political, and intellectual developments of history to God's Kingdom even when these efforts stress the transcendent and even apocalyptic aspects of the Kingdom far more than the social gospel ever did. However, there are also objections based on reason, and others which are based on faith.

As far as reason is concerned, it apparently is impossible for many theologians to think that modern man can conceive of history as ending objectively in any other way than that suggested by the scientists when they speak of the inevitable extinction of human life resulting from the explosion or dying of the sun, the operations of the second law of thermodynamics, the collapse of an oscillating universe or some other natural cause. However, when one thinks of the appeal of science fiction, of Marxist Utopian myths, or even of Teilhard de Chardin, one becomes very wary of pontificating about what modern man can or cannot believe. It is doubtful, contrary to what many intellectualistic, academic theologians seem to think, that we are moving into a period when world pictures are less indispensible and less mythical (though, to be sure, the myths must now be related to science) than in the past.

Another objection is more specifically theological and for our purposes, therefore, more serious. It is that any kind of objectivizing thinking, including the attribution of an objectively future dimension to eschatology, is dangerous for faith. It threatens to substitute belief in what purport to be objectively true doctrines for that radical risk of decision, for that total openness to God's future, for that personal authenticity and existential engagement which is the essence of biblical eschatology and Christian faith. After all, so the argument goes, the heart of the New Testament message is concerned with man's decision in the present for or against the New Age which has begun in Christ. Nothing can be allowed to distract from this. What does the future redemption of humanity profit if human beings lose their lives in the here and now?

The Reformation provenance of this kind of objection is evident. It is a transposition into a modern idiom of the *sola fide*. However, it is at the same time obvious that the sixteenth-century Reformers did not have the distaste for objectivities as do so many of their modern disciples. They believed that historical faith, that intellectual assent to the objective truth of the resurrection and the future judgment, for example, was involved in saving faith, in *fiducia*. For them, as is quite clear from the Lutheran confessional writings, the peculiarly Reformation emphases, such as justification *sola fide* were necessary correctives of the distortions which had crept into the Catholic tradition and not at all meant to be constitutive of a basically new understanding of Christianity as many contemporary Protestants, existentialist and non-existentialist, suppose. There can, I suppose, be no doubt that, while those who reject eschatological objectivity are more insistent on what is specifically Protestant, those who accept it are more faithful to the total thinking of the Reformers, which, after all, remained basically catholic.

In short, what I have called the objective version of the eschatological-historical outlook transcends the confessional boundaries. It is neither specifically Catholic nor Protestant, and it provides a new common framework for the discussion of the

traditional differences in a way which a purely existential theology, for example, cannot do.

IV

In conclusion, then, I would like to indicate with untoward
brevity four points of *rapprochement* within this new framework, and then comment on one continuing, though transformed, area of disagreement.

The first point is of central importance from the Protestant
side, but it has already been mentioned and so can be quickly
dealt with. When eschatological categories are used, particularly
when these are combined with a personalistic and existential in-
sight into the historicity of human life, the old theological conflicts over the *sola fide* and the *sola gratia,* over free will and
predestination, over sin and concupiscence, simply disappear. A
great deal more work needs to be done before this is clear in all
its details, but the general outlines of the reconciliation are already apparent. Both Catholics and Protestants are regaining
the biblical view of salvation as the passage from the old to the
coming age, or release from bondage to demonic powers into
the freedom of the sons of God, of deliverance from that fixa-
tion on the past which leads to attempts at self-justification
into openness to God's future. On neither side can we debate
the old issues in terms of that individualism which we inherited
from Augustine perhaps more than anyone else, and which alone
made meaningful the disputes over, for example, infused grace
versus the external imputation of righteousness.

The overcoming of the individualism of the Western tradition
calls our attention to a second area of *rapprochement,* this
time ecclesial. Not only the Bible, but also history and sociology,
have made us far more conscious of the social nature of man
than even Aristotle was in the past. Oddly enough, on this point
the extreme theological existentialists, with their ignoring of